LANGUAGE

and

ESOL

METHODOLOGY

- a unique perspective

IRWIN GOLDSTEIN

PARTRIDGE

A Penguin Random House Company

To order additional copies of this book, contact
Toll Free 800 101 2657 (Singapore)
Toll Free 1 800 81 7340 (Malaysia)
orders.singapore@partridgepublishing.com

www.partridgepublishing.com/singapore

CONTENTS

ABOUT THE AUTHOR

Dr. Irwin Goldstein

A distinguished career in the field of teaching and administration began in 1959. When attending Oswego State Teachers' College in Oswego, New York, the author chose to do his student teaching at the Onondaga Indian Reservation in Nedrow, New York. The culture of the Native Americans which he experienced first hand had an important impact on his future professional choices. He went on to obtain a Master of Science degree in education from Hunter College in New York City and later a doctorate degree in Education and Administration from Yeshiva University.

He served as an elementary and junior high school teacher in New York City public schools, where he worked extensively with minority ESOL (English for Students of Other Languages) students from many different countries and cultures. As a result of his successful innovative work with multiethnic children during the daytime, he was offered an additional evening position as an ESOL teacher of adults. This led to his appointment as supervisor of instruction, and later as assistant director of the citywide federally funded adult education program.

In addition, Dr. Goldstein worked closely with Jim Hall, President of York College in N.Y.C., teaching, training staff and developing the college's ESOL program. In the 1970s he was appointed coordinator of the Jersey City College Right to Read Program. Besides supervising the program's instructional activities, volunteer training, and maintaining ongoing contact with community groups and service agencies, he gave special attention to adults in the community who were in need of English language instruction. Later, at the urging of Rabbi Morris Sherer, he accepted the position of Education Director of Project COPE (Career Opportunities and Preparation for Employment), a division of Agudath Israel of America. Many hundreds of Russian immigrants were serviced in the area of ESOL under his supervision. Dr. Goldstein had a marked impact on ESOL instruction while building and improving the programs.

His other activities included serving as a member of New York State's Commissioner of Education Gordon Ambach's Bilingual Education and Adult Learning Services Councils. Besides that, he was instrumental in establishing the Council of American Immigrant Agencies (a consortium of multiple ethnic agencies in New York City), and serving as a consultant to the New York City Board of Education's Instructional Management Program

The current work was written by Dr. Goldstein in clear understandable English to share his experience and knowledge of ESOL methodology and related matters with teachers and lay people everywhere who are interested in the field.

PREFACE

Through the years in discussions with numerous well-meaning individuals, I have found that many misconceptions exist regarding teaching English to non-English speakers. For example, just because one can read one is not by that criterion alone capable of teaching reading. In the same way, knowing a particular language well does not ensure the adequate teaching of it. It is an error to assume that common sense alone can guide one to teach a language such as English to others. What some may consider common sense may in actuality not be. Common sense is simply not as common as might be believed. In ESOL teaching what may appear as a sensible thing to do may in fact (as the material in the text will show) prove counter-productive and, in turn, detrimental to the learning process.

Another factor to consider is the narrow focus some instructors bring to the teaching process. Failure to see beyond one's own artificial horizon limits an educator's ability to be eclectic and maximally effective. Clichés such as "There are no bad students, only bad teachers" arise from instructor inflexibility. It is important that an ESOL teacher grow familiar with varied methods and philosophies, rather than relying on only one. In ESOL teaching, one size does not fit all. An approach or method which works well with some students may have to be greatly modified or even replaced to teach others effectively.

Consider for example viewing a work of art such as Leonardo Di Vinci's *MonaLisa*. It is generally known that it is her smile which brings mystique to the work. If, however, the viewer focuses only upon the smile and neglects all other aspects of the painting, they will miss the indubitable magnitude of the work. They will not be aware that the artist utilized a pyramid design in which he placed the model. They will not notice the geometry of circles and spheres on the paintings' surfaces. They will miss inspecting the landscape in the background which some contend was influenced by Chinese paintings. The armrest on the chair in which the Mona Lisa sits, which serves as an element of division between her and the viewer, as well as the model's erect posture, her folded arms, and her gaze which appears fixed on the viewer will pass them by. In addition, they will not see the model in a comprehensive way. They will, therefore, not be inclined to ask such questions as, "Was the woman who posed for Leonardo's painting chosen because she was beautiful?" "Were her looks perceived as beauty in the 15th century?" "Could it have been that she was not considered beautiful at all, but that the artist chose to paint her in a realistic way, not as a beauty but as she was?"

Both a broad as well as a circumscribed view which converge to produce a suitably harmonious understanding of what is seen is what one should strive for. My writing is therefore designed to reflect a broad outlook, as well as a detailed examination of certain aspects of language and ESOL methodology. As a result, a panoramic view of language in general and of ESOL teaching approaches is included in the current work. I have also focused on a detailed description of one teaching method which has had a particularly strong impact on ESOL instruction. Also to be addressed are early ESOL testing development, and how decisions are sometimes made regarding the use of tests and their impact on many programs.

The reader should keep in mind that the ideas and suggestions proposed in this work pertaining to the teaching of ESOL are only recommendations and are hence subject to interpretation. Nevertheless, practitioners should feel free to draw upon them as an aid to help improve teaching methods.

CHAPTER 1

What Is Language?

If one is interested in helping others to learn an additional language, it is useful to clarify what language actually is. We often use terms whose meanings we are confident of, yet if asked to define, we find it a cause for pause.

United States Supreme Court Justice Potter Stewart in attempting to define "pornography" in a 1964 obscenity case, made the following well-known remark: "I shall not today attempt further to define the kind of material I understand to be embraced . . . but I know it when I see it." In this sense, it is apparent that most people feel they know quite well what language is but find it difficult to define. In actuality there are numerous definitions of language. Some that Webster's *New World Dictionary* lists are:

- "The expression of thoughts and feelings by means of vocal sounds, and combinations of such sounds to which meaning is attributed: human speech."
- "Any means of expressing or communicating as gestures, signs, animal sounds, and so on."
- "All the vocal sounds, words and the ways of combining them common to a particular nation, tribe or other group."

- "The particular term or manner of selecting and combining words characteristic of a person, group, and so on."

The *American Heritage Dictionary* cites other definitions, including:

- "Communication of thoughts and feelings through a system of arbitrary signals such as voice sounds, gestures or written symbols."

Mary Finocchiaro includes these definitions in her publication:[1]

- "Language is the means by which results of human thought and action are passed on."
- "Language is learned behavior."

And the one she finds preferable:

- "Language is a system of arbitrary, vocal symbols which permits all people in a given culture, or other people who have learned the system of that culture, to communicate or to interact."

UnixL presents yet another definition.[2] It tells us that language is:

- "a system of communicating with other people using sounds, symbols, and words in communications as well as using expressions through body language."

---

[1] Finocchiaro, M. (1974). Motivation in Language Learning. CATESOL Occasional Papers, No. 5 [microform].

[2] UnixL search http://www.unixl.com/dir/education/languages/language_definition and phrases in a particular language convey the meanings they do, speakers of every language understand and use the words and phrases in their language to function and to express themselves.

If one searches, many additional definitions will surface. The purpose is not, however, to locate or analyze every definition of language. Suffice it to say that there are many. Although there are differences among the definitions, all have merit and certain key elements in common. Rather than viewing them as being in conflict with one another and, as a consequence, a stumbling block to understanding what language truly is, it is more productive to accept them as different ways of characterizing language. In this sense, all the above definitions may be considered suitable for the purpose of this writing. Since the material being presented will view multiple aspects of language, none of the definitions should be disregarded. The reader should keep in mind that one definition may apply to a particular topic under discussion more so than another.

It is noteworthy that the term *arbitrary* is not uncommon in language definitions. A view relating to a biblical interpretation will be shown, which suggests that originally it was known why words expressed what they did and that they were not selected arbitrarily. Today, however, most would concur that in a later development of language expansion, certain words and phrases were randomly chosen and later spread and became acceptable. Why for example in English does the word *dog* refer to the animal it does? Why does *apricot* mean a particular fruit? Words such as these, according to the language definitions which use the term *arbitrary*, were selected by some notion or whim which 'caught on' so to speak, and they were soon adopted by all speakers of that language.

This holds true too for rules used to position words in phrases and sentences, such as *a radio car* versus *a car radio*. In other words, according to the definitions under discussion, such rules for positioning also developed in an arbitrary manner. Although it is not known why words and phrases in a particular language convey the meanings they do speakers of every language understand and use the words and phrases in their language to function and express themselves.

In terms of the definitions of language in general, helpful as they are in conveying an idea of what language is considered to be, they do not include a detailed discussion of the components

3

and subdivisions of language or of its skills areas. These topics can be delineated as follows:

Elements of Language and Their Components

The basic components of English and all languages are:

I.   Sound system
II. Structure
III. Vocabulary

I. The Sound System

The major elements of the Sound System are:

Intonation, which is the rise and fall of the voice in a sentence, such as questions where the voice rises and statements where the voice falls or is kept level.

Stress, which is the emphasis of certain words in a sentence, as well as the loudness and softness of the voice:

EXAMPLE: Are the chil dren playing?

versus

Are the children pla ying?

Stress also involves accentuation when a single word is concerned:

EXAMPLE: pre sent versus present

Rhythm, which is the 'music' of language and involves the interval of time between beats in a sentence

EXAMPLE: English elongation

"How are you?" [youuu?] where the word **you** is extended versus a staccato rendition of the same words, "How ar' yú?"

Pronunciation, which is the placing of the tongue and lips, and involves the voice box

Alphabet Utilization for Pronunciation

In ESOL teaching the alphabet cannot be used as an absolute guide for pronunciation. This is because the same letter sometimes produces a different sound:

- The letter /c/ sound in **cat** versus its sound in **certain**
- The letter /s/ sound in **see** versus its sound in **sugar**

Phonemes and Allophones

In pronunciation too phonemes and allophones play a role. Phonemes are sounds in a language which differentiate between meanings. Every language has sounds which do not exist in some other languages. Students learning English, whose native language does not have certain English sounds, tend to substitute the closest sound in their native language for the correct English sound. Either they do not actually hear the sound (since it does not exist for them in the language they know), or they hear it but are unable at first to produce it correctly. In the Spanish language, for example, the /y/ sound as in *yellow* or the /i/ sound as in *ship* do not exist. It is therefore not unusual for Spanish speakers learning English to replace the /y/ sound with a /j/ and to inadvertently produce a word with an entirely different meaning:

For the word *yellow*, they might substitute *jello*.

For the word *ship*, it is not uncommon for them to say *sheep*.

Many other examples of phoneme difficulties are commonly encountered by non-English speakers: h*iss* instead of *his, some* instead of *sun,* n*od* instead of *not*, and so on.

Each native language poses its own challenges to students learning English as an additional language.

Allophones are variant sounds of a phoneme which do not differentiate between meanings. For example, English speakers rarely recognize that the /p/ sound in the word *pie* is not the same as the /p/ sound in *lip*. Although the use of either /p/ sound in English does not alter the meaning of any English word (therefore in English it is an allophone), such a difference might indeed affect word meanings in another language.

Voiced and Voiceless Sounds

In pronunciation there are also voiced and voiceless sounds. In a voiced sound, the producer's vocal cords vibrate. This, for example, holds true for the /z/ sound in English. If a sound is voiceless, one feels no vocal cord vibration as in production of the voiceless s sound. By placing one's finger on the gullet or the throat, the vibration of the /z/ sound and lack of any vibration of the s sound can be clearly felt.

II. Structure

The key elements of the structure of language are **inflections**, **word order** and **function words.**

Inflections are the change in the form of a word to indicate plurality or possession. Examples of these are:

Country to **countries**

David to **David's**

Word order determines the meaning of a group of words. Knowing the meaning of each word in a phrase or sentence is often not enough to determine its meaning. The same group of words in another order may give the phrase or sentence an entirely different meaning. Examples of this are: *The dog bit the man* versus *The man bit the dog.* Or a *radio car* versus a *car radio*. Or the d*oor lock* versus *Lock the door.* Or a *pen light* versus a *light pen*.

Function words in English are words with little or no meaning by themselves but which are used in utterances to signal grammatical relationships. Auxiliaries and prepositions possess this quality. Examples are: **is, the, at, or, are, for, which, from** and **by**.

III.   Vocabulary

Vocabulary consists of the lexical items or lexicon of a language. These are generally content words which refer to things, actions or qualities.

Although there is little dispute on what the components and subdivisions of language are, there is little unanimity of opinion on the most effective way to help students acquire a new language such as English. Through the years numerous teaching methods have emerged and have been employed. As a result of various factors, such as the development of new language learning theories and research findings, many of the former teaching methods were partially, if not fully, abandoned. Others were modified in keeping with up-to-date linguistic development or current language learning discoveries. In a later section, some of the methods related to English language teaching and their current status will be addressed.

The Skills Areas of Language

Webster (*New World Dictionary*) defines "skill" as "distinction" and "the ability to separate" as well as "ability in a particular area." Most languages consist of four skill areas which are:

- Listening
- Speaking
- Reading
- Writing

Although almost all languages may be said to share all of these skills, there are exceptions in which only listening and speaking comprise the language. Examples are:

- The Piraha language, which is spoken by a hunter-gatherer tribe of Amazon Indians who number about 350 people. They reside alongside the Maici River, a tributary of theAmazon River in Brazil.
- The Burushaski language, which is predominantly oral. (The Arabic alphabet is sometimes used to record aspects of it, but no fixed orthography exists.). It is used by over 87,000 speakers located in areas near and in Pakistan and Kashmir.
- The Koro language of India is spoken by over 1,000 people who live in a remote Indian village called Kichang.

The lack of reading and writing skills in some, even if in relatively few languages, serves to emphasize the significance of speech. Speech is a phenomenon unique to human beings and a characteristic which separates man from other species. Despite animal communications among themselves through sounds such as grunts and moans, such communications differ from human speech in which individuals express their ideas, thoughts and feelings through words. Unlike other species, however, nowhere in the entire world do people exist without a spoken language.

Some Shared Traits of Language

Besides most languages sharing the skills enumerated above, all languages may be said to have certain traits in common. *Trait* is defined by Webster (*New World Dictionary*) as "a distinguishing quality or characteristic."

One important trait shared by languages is that the social environment and culture of its users can be detected through any of them. If there are many lexical items which relate to an item or issue, it is an indication that users of that language attach significance to it in their habitat. American English, for example, consists of a vast vocabulary related to money matters and finance. People often discuss the stock market, worker and executive salaries and income, unemployment insurance, minimum wages, pensions, social security, loans, mortgages, credit, interest rates, savings, taxes and so on. Such a focus conveys an aspect of citizens' interest which is linked to the USA culture and environment. To the extent that other English speaking countries exhibit a similar focus in such matters, the same may be said to hold true for them.

Another example consists of the many lexical items in American English which refer to those in need of assistance. A small sampling of such words is: handicapped, invalid, disabled, mentally or physically challenged, disadvantaged, underprivileged, indigent, impoverished, homeless, incapacitated, destitute, slow (as in learning), special (as in "special needs children"), infirm and so on.

In other parts of the world, such as where the Inuit and Yupik peoples dwell (terms they prefer to Eskimo), the language spoken differentiates between types of snow. Many words for it exist. This is due to the sensitivity and ability of these people to recognize that not all snow is the same for them, and that different kinds affect their lives in different ways. Snow has a major effect on their social organization and is reflective of an important element of their culture. This is discerned through an examination of their language.

A second existing trait shared by all languages is that each has a system to discuss present, past and future happenings.

Still another is that although every language is limited in the amount of sounds it possesses, there is no limit to the amount of words and expressions that speakers of that language can develop with its sounds. The sounds can be joined in multiple unions to produce whatever words or sayings are needed for communication. All languages also have a set of rules. The latter permit language users to express their views and ideas, ask questions and relate information about themselves, others and things they consider important. In addition, all languages are capable of allowing their users to function adequately in everyday life. The vocabulary needed for people to carry on with what and whom they encounter in their daily lives is sufficient in every language. New encounters or objects which enter a community from afar or through discovery call for new words or expressions. These are sometimes borrowed from another language community and incorporated into one's own. They might also be modified creatively by the new users. In Israel, for example, where Modern Hebrew is spoken, the term *back axle* (for a vehicle) was borrowed from English. From this, however, the front axle of a vehicle came to be called *front back axle*. In Hebrew too a bus is not simply referred to as a *bus*. It is more properly designated as an *auto bus*.

Section Summary

In this section various definitions of language were presented with the view that although differences exist among them, they all possess some validity, and that each definition might best apply to different aspects of the discussion on language. The components, skills and traits of language were also delineated and discussed. These factors, it was pointed out, can be considered common to all languages. In the forthcoming section various theories pertaining to the origin of language will be examined.

CHAPTER 2

The Mystery of the Origin of Language

Two outlooks essentially encompass the theories related to the origin of languages. On one hand there is the Creationist or biblical explanation of how language originated. On the other hand, there are attempts to explain this phenomenon without biblical reference. For those who subscribe to the biblical outlook, there is no mystery to language origin. For those who seek other answers, however, the picture is more complex. The latter group often concludes and refers to the origin of language as an unsolved mystery.

A. A Biblical Perspective

If one explores the origin of language, one finds the earliest account in the Book of Genesis of the Hebrew Bible. This description indicates that in the beginning, language neither evolved nor was it arbitrary. What is further evidential from the biblical account is that G-d embedded language in man when he was created, rather than man having invented language. "And out of the ground G-d formed every beast of the field and every bird of the sky and brought them to man to see what he would call them. Whatever man called a living thing, that was to be its name. And the man gave names to the fowl of the sky and to every beast of the field." (Genesis 2:19-20). Rabbi Yaakov Culi in his commentary on these verses emphasizes that Adam gave each creature a name. In many cases the male was designated a name which differed from the female. He stresses that Adam was able to do this "because he understood the essential nature of every creature." He did not choose names arbitrarily since, if this were so, the text would not have conveyed the idea that each living creature was given a name. Adam in terms of the account, therefore, had a reason for each name he used. There are those who maintain that to the present day the Hebrew name of every creature is the one that Adam originally gave it. The commentary continues with "God then asked him (Adam) 'And what shall be your own name?' When he produced the name Adam, G-d said, "I find Adam to be an appropriate name. You were taken from the ground [which in Hebrew is *adamah*]."[3] So we find in this narrative a portrayal of the first man's possession of and ability to understand and use language without it having been taught him or without it having evolved.

In conjunction with the above a theory also exists, although disputed, that Hebrew was the first language and that all other languages developed or are derived from it.[4] Some refer to the language spoken by Adam and Eve as the Adamic language and use the term as a synonym for Hebrew. Others maintain it was not identical to Hebrew. Perhaps what was spoken in Eden was a pre-biblical Hebrew. Adam's descendants may have preserved it to an extent, but it may have begun to evolve naturally as all languages do. The Old English, for example, used at the time the epic poem *Beowolf* was written (sometime between the 7th and 8th centuries) was quite different from English in the time of Shakespeare (16th and 17th centuries). Modern English in turn differs significantly from the English of the Shakespearean era. The Talmud tells us only that "the Torah was written in the vernacular of the Jews" (*Talmud Sanhedrin* 21b). Because the vernacular at the time was used in the writing of the Torah

---

[3]   Culi, Yaakov. (1988). *The Torah analogy Genesis 1*, Moznaim, New York, Jerusalem.

[4]   Hebrew Language—Love to Know. Classic Encyclopedia based on the 11th edition of the Encyclopedia Britannica, 1911. Jenkins, Orville B., "Hebrew—the Original Language? (Of Course Not!). Retrieved from Thoughts and Resources, December 21, 2004.

(the five books of Moses), it is termed *Loshen HaKodesh* or the Holy Language. One might argue that although biblical Hebrew contained many elements of the Adamic language, it was not identical with it.[5]

Extrapolations from current languages are sometimes employed in an attempt to shed light on languages used in the past or to gain greater insight into certain aspects of the influence one language may have had upon others. In Hebrew, for example, the name Adam gave his mate Hava (Eve) is derived from or at least closely related to the word *hai*, which means life. As mentioned previously, the name Adam, which he gave himself, means ground or earth. These names only have meaning in Hebrew. Such factors, some maintain, are clues indicating that the Bible regards the Hebrew language, or at least a form of it, as having been the original language of mankind. This idea is also conveyed in the *Midrash* which states, "Just as the Torah was given in Hebrew, so was the world created with Hebrew." (Midrash Rabbah, Genesis 30:8)

The theory that other languages developed from or were influenced by Hebrew is also derived by a form of extrapolation. If one compares the names of the Hebrew and Greek alphabet letters, for example, a similarity is clearly seen.

The Hebrew names of the letters such as alef, bait (or bet), gimmel, daled are close to the Greek pronunciations alpha, beta, gamma, delta. In Greek, however, the letters are only sounds. Their names have no intrinsic meaning. In other words, the Greek letters are arbitrary symbols. In Hebrew, however, every letter has at least a single meaning in its own right. Most are in fact viewed as having multiple meanings. Outside of Chinese ideograms or Egyptian hieroglyphics in which pictures or symbols rather than alphabet letters are used to represent words or sounds, there appears to be no other language other than Hebrew which possesses meanings for all of its alphabet letters. Proponents of this view suggest that the meanings of the Hebrew alphabet letters are derived from such factors as their sound, their contour or the unmasking of each letter's

---

[5]   Olender, M. (December 1977). From the language of Adam to the Pluralism of Babel. Mediterranean Historical *Review*, *12* (2), 51-59.

inner message. Rabbi Yitzchak Ginsburgh postulates that the word(s) stemming from each Hebrew letter are as follows:[6]

Letter	Word (s)	Word Linkage Example (using single word)
Alef	Oxen; thousand; teaching; master	**Master** of the Universe—G-d
Beit	House	**House** of G-d—holy Temple
Gimmel	Bridge; weaning; benevolence	**Bridge**: the shape of the gimmel merges two areas (opposing forces) into one. Related to word *gamla*, a bridge which unites two areas.
Dalet	Door, poor man; lifting up; elevation	**Door** one opens in oneself to needs of fellow human being
Hei	To be broken; to take seed; behold—revelation	**Revelation**: seeing beyond as through a window—understanding teaching of G-d
Vav	Hook	**Hook**: connection of man to G-d
Zayin	Weapon—sword; ornament or grown; species—gender, to sustain	**Sustain** spiritual values as does a "woman of valor"
Chet	Fear; life—whose full expression is love	**Life** force within one's body
Tet	Inclination; staff-snake; below; bed	**Inclination** towards goodness and repentance
Yud	Hand; to thrust	**Hand**: power and possession
Kaf	Palm; clouds; power to suppress	**Palm** outstretched to help the poor, the needy

---

6   Ginsburgh, Y. (1990). *The Hebrew letters: Channels of creative consciousness*, Gal Einai, Jerusalem.

Lamed	To learn; to teach	To **learn** and **teach** G-d's word
Mem	Water; blemish	**Water** as in the sea or fountain of wisdom
Nun	Fish; kingdom; heir to throne	**Fish** as a symbol to propagate offspring as **heir** to the throne—Messiah
Samech	To support; rely on; ordination	**Support** of the Divine
Ayin	Eye; color; foundation	**Eye**: sight and insight
Pei	Mouth; here (present)	**Mouth**: as organ of speech—to communicate oral law
Tzadik	A tzadik (righteous individual); to hunt	**To hunt** for lost souls and make them righteous
Kuf	Monkey; to surround or touch; strength	**To surround:** go around as in word h*akapah*, namely, cycles of nature.
Reish	Head or beginning; poor man	**Beginning** of understanding—clarification
Shin	A year; a tooth; scarlet; serenity; to sleep	**Tooth:** crushes, grinds food making it digestible—related to integrating G-d's teachings.
Tav	Sign; impression; code	**Seal** of G-d (which will not be changed)

One must not dismiss out of hand as implausible the idea that all languages stem from a single early language or a proto-world language.[7] Recent scientific research of mitochondrial DNA from cells of diversified racial communities, for example, suggests weighty backing for the assumption that all people are descended from the same genetic ancestry.[8] If originally the

---

[7]   Rohde, D.L., Olson, S. & Chang J.T (2004). Modeling the recent common ancestry of all living humans. *Nature Journal, 431,* 562-566.

[8]   Watts, M. H. (1998). *The Lord gave the word: A study in the history of the biblical text.* London, England:

limited number of people that existed functioned in a particular language, a case can be made that all languages today are derived from the same language.

Continuing with the biblical narrative, Genesis gives an account of the Tower of Babel which tends to explain both small and vast differences in languages.

"And the whole earth was one language and of one speech. 2. And it came to pass, as they journeyed east, that they found a plain in the land of Shinar; and they dwelt there. 3. And they said one to another: 'Come, let us make brick, and burn them thoroughly.' And they had brick for stone, and slime had they for mortar. 4. And they said: come, let us build us a city, and a tower, with its top in heaven, and let us make us a name; lest we be scattered abroad upon the face of the whole earth.' 5. And the Lord came down to see the city and the tower, which the children of men builded. 6. And the Lord said: 'Behold, they are one people, and they have all one language; and this is what they begin to do; and now nothing will be withholden from them, which they purpose to do. 7. Come, let us go down, and there confound their language, that they may not understand one another's speech.' 8. So the Lord scattered them abroad from thence upon the face of all the earth; and they left off to build the city. 9. Therefore was the name of it called Babel; because the Lord did there confound the language of all the earth; and from thence did the Lord scatter them abroad upon the face of all the earth." (Genesis 11:1-9)

The variety of languages is, therefore, traced to a time of 340 years after the great flood. According to biblical calculation, the flood occurred in the year 2107 BCE. The scattering of the Babel tower builders took place in 1764 BCE. G-d blamed the builders for not having learned the lesson of those who were destroyed by the relatively recent flood for their sins and viewed the construction of the tower as a rebellion against him.[9] Hence, according to the Bible, language diversity came about as a punishment by G-d.

---

[9]   Culi, pp.412-413

Some maintain that those who descended from one of Noah's sons, Yafet (Japhet), prior to the Tower of Babel story in the Bible, spoke different languages. "Of these were the isles of the nations divided in their lands, every one after his tongue, after their families in their nations." (Genesis 10:15). That there were different languages in Yafet's times is considered erroneous by traditional Hebrew biblical commentators. For example, Dr. J. H. Hertz in the introduction to his *Pentateuch* explains that scriptural narratives are not always placed in chronological order. "Sometimes an event is anticipated, at other times it is told in connection with a later event."

That Hertz does not translate the Hebrew *eesh l'lshono* used in the Yafet narration as *language* but rather as *tongue*, while translating the Hebrew word *sofo* as language in the Tower of Babel description, may be consistent with a similar analysis by Rabbi Samson Raphael Hirsch. Hirsch maintains that different dialects rather than different languages had evolved by the Yafet period. At that time, he asserts, all people continued to function in a single language. He translates the Hebrew *eesh l'lshono* as "to each his dialect." He points out, "There appears to be a clear-cut difference between *sofo*, the term used in the account of the next development (the Tower of Babel) and *loshon*, the term used in the present chapter (Yafet). *Sofo* denotes language as in German, French, and so on, while *loshon* refers to manner of speech, pronunciation or dialect."[10] 10

Different dialects may have served to separate groups into different commonwealths, but their use of the same languages served as an important link or bond between them. Such connections were, of course, severed after the Tower of Babel.

B. An Alternative Approach

Many scholars are skeptical of the biblical account of the origin of language. However, all would likely agree that there is no alternative explanation based on empirical scientific

[10] Rabbi Samson Raphael Hirsch, S.R. Rabbi. (1990).*The Pentateuch Trumath Tzvi* (p.51, footnote 2). New York: Judaica Press.

research which is not open to major criticism and doubt. A primary difficulty of those who seek alternative explanations and empirical evidence of language origin is the dilemma they are confronted with pertaining to language continuity. Since language is not inborn, humans must be exposed to a language before acquiring it. Evolutionary theories of language development simply do not lend themselves to empirical observation. Although evolutionists speculate that at some stage the human brain was altered so that language creation was made possible (a language acquisition device evolved), this does not explain what the first language was or how it developed. Nor does it address the question of why there are so many languages.

In the 19th century several hypotheses attempted to explain language origin. Otto Jeperson, a critic of these hypotheses who believed they were invalid speculation, originally gave them cynical names to ridicule them. Ironically, the names not only stuck but were imitated in style in the naming of new hypotheses. Some of the early concepts were:

The **Ding-Dong** theory:

This theory postulates that language started when people associated the natural sounds they heard with particular objects, behavior or events and verbally imitated these sounds.

Onomatopoeia then is considered the key element in how language began. If one uses English as an illustration of the onomatopoeia concept of language origin, an example would be the word *jingle* which mimics the sound beads make when shaken. According to the theory, the first language developed by these types of associations. The Ding-Dong hypothesis is viewed as having little credibility since the number of words in a given language which imitate sounds is very limited. In addition, it does not account for the names given to natural noiseless entities such as the sun, a stone, caring, sanity, courage, bravery and the like. Other theories in the same category were also dismissed as hardly relevant with more or less similar criticisms. They include:

The **Pooh-Pooh** theory:

This theory posits that words originated from man's feelings of sighs of pleasure, means of pain, yelps of surprise, cries of sorrow, and so on.

The **Bow-Wow** theory:

This theory suggests that man began to speak by mimicking animal sounds.

The **Ta-Ta** theory

This theory ties the beginning of language to body movement (parroting). There have also been theories and hypotheses that early man's need to communicate while hunting was responsible for language origin. Critics of such ideas point out that hunting generally requires silence rather than vocal articulation. Furthermore, animals also hunt without possessing a language of speech. Through the years more sophisticated theories were introduced, but all had major flaws. Some were judged to have faults similar to, if not identical, to their earlier counterparts.

In 1866 a significant development occurred. The prestigious Linguistic Society of Paris concluded that hypotheses and theories on the origin of language would always encounter scientific skepticism and doubt. As a result, the society declared that the question of how language originated was unanswerable. It refused to allow further discussion or accept any papers on this topic (Vajda, 2010). In 1872 the London Philological Society took an almost identical stand. It concluded that different origin of language hypotheses could not be ranked scientifically against one another. It too suspended dialogue and deliberation on the issue of language origin.[11]

Despite these events the debate continued and is with us to the present day. In modern times, no new theory has been recognized or accepted as a consensual answer. It is not surprising then that prominent scholars in the field see little hope of finding a solution. Noam Chomsky, for example, a recognized expert in the field, postulates that all human beings are born with a hard-voiced language acquisition device (LAD) in the brain. They are born, he speculates, with principles of language, a sort of universal grammar in place but must frame many parameters to learn a language. Chomsky concurs that this does not answer the question of language origin. In referring to the status of researchers resolving the issue, he said, "Very few people are concerned with the origin of language because most consider it a hopeless question."[12] Aichison (2000) summarized the issue as follows: "Of course holes still remain in our knowledge, in particular, at which stage did language leap from being something new which humans discovered to being something which every newborn human is scheduled to acquire. This is still a puzzle."

[11] Corballis, M. (2008) Not the last word [Review of the book *The first word: The search for the origins of language*, by C. Kenneally]. *American Scientist, 96*(1), 68.

[12] Ross, P. E. (1991). Hard words. *Scientific American Magazine, 264* (4), 138-147.

CHAPTER 3

The Development of the English Language

Language does not remain static but is in a continuous, though gradual, state of change. Over long periods of time, vast changes are clearly evident. This means that earlier versions of a modern language are hardly recognizable as the same language by current users. The English language is no exception to this criterion.

In approximately 4,500 C.E., several German tribes including Anglos and Saxons made their way to eastern and southern England. The Celts who lived there prior to the arrival of the tribes were in turn mostly displaced. The dialects from these various groups were mainly German coupled with some Latin, which the educated population, most of them clergy, knew well. This combination resulted in what is today called Old English or Anglo Saxon. It was spoken until the mid-twelfth century. English speakers today might recognize some of the lexical items but would be hard pressed to decipher the meaning of a verbal or written Old English work. This is the language in which the poem *Beowulf* was written. The following is an example taken from the beginning of the poem.

Old English	Freely Translated
Hwaet! We Gar-Dengin in gear. daguum peadcyninga, prym gefranon, ho oa aepelingas ellen fremedons	Lo! We have heard about the might of the spear—Danes' kings in the early days and how those heroes promoted zeal.

As time moved on, additional groups entered the country speaking other languages. When the Norsemen and Danes entered England at the start of the ninth century, their phrases and vocabulary merged with Old English. The language soon consisted of an Anglo-Saxon base with words borrowed from Danish and other Scandinavian languages as well as Latin. Words of Latin origin such as cup, cheese, kitchen, candle and angel stem from this merger.

Further changes occurred when the French, under William the Conqueror, subdued England in 1066. So many French words penetrated the language that it developed into what is known today as Middle English. This is the language used by Geoffrey Chaucer (1343-1400), noted poet and writer of the time, who became known as the father of English literature. In the fifteenth century many more Latin and Greek words were absorbed by the language. Middle English lasted until approximately the sixteenth century.

Factors such as the merging of different dialects, regional speech differences, accents, new word adoptions and creations, novel expressions, new pronunciations, and so on contributed more and more to changes in language sounds. This continued until Middle English was replaced by Early Modern English. The time period in which Early Modern English was used ranged from the beginning of the sixteenth century to approximately the middle of the seventeenth. The works of William Shakespeare (born in 1564) were developed during this time. Since then, the English we currently use and are most familiar with is referred to as Modern English.

English today is the lingua franca of the world. It is estimated that approximately 380 million native English speakers exist. In addition, probably as many as a billion people use English as a second language. English has interacted with many different languages, has affected them and has in turn been influenced by them.

Many words in English were borrowed from other languages such as Greek, Latin, French, German, the Aztec Indian language, Sanskrit from India, Portuguese, Spanish and so on.

Many of the scientific terms we use in English today, such as astronomy, geology and biology, were borrowed from the Greek and Latin. Other words related to sports, mythology, politics and religion, such as gymnasium, Amazon, democracy, bishop and Catholic also came to English from Greek and Latin. The vocabulary of English is the largest of any language which exists. In the time of old English, Christian missionaries brought the Latin alphabet to England from Ireland. It has obviously been retained as the English system of writing.[13]

By no means should we imagine that the English language used today is no longer subject to dramatic change. On the contrary, as was noted earlier, the tendency of language is to be altered by usage. Language is simply not a fixed entity, neither is it immutable. It is in fact a dynamic property which continues to grow, develop and change.

Today we are living in the rocket age. Although change always occurred in the past, it appears that not only are greater changes occurring in our time but that they are proceeding at an accelerated pace. Note for example the sudden collapse of the former Soviet Union or the disappearance of the Berlin Wall and the rapid reunification of East and West Germany. Note also the unexpected emergence of radical Islam and such factors as the abrupt decline of the United States economy and that of other countries. Swift and dramatic happenings in English language usage are making their mark too, besides the slower changes which might have been anticipated. New forms of expressions are created by the Internet and text-messaging that were unknown several years ago. Both written and oral language is affected by such developments. The new technology is used by

---

[13] Killoran, Nial. (n.d.). Old English, Anglo-Saxon (Englisc). *Omniglot, the Online Encyclopedia of Writing Systems and Language.* Retrieved from www.omniglot.com/writing/oldenglish.htm

some, especially by the younger generation, to rapidly spread innovative oral utterances, slang remarks, unusual expressions and new ways of communicating graphically to vast numbers of others. In the process, conventional grammar, such as the use of capital letters (when for example surfing the Internet) and spelling practices (such as when texting or twittering) are altered, if not entirely disregarded. Inventive spellings such as "*u*" for "*you*" or words used to replace customary vocabulary, such as renaming the punctuation mark word "*period*" by referring to it as "*dot*" at the end of a sentence, are now common among teenagers. Whether one is pleased by such language manipulation, because it is novel and creative, or appalled because it is primitive and destructive, many of these variations will likely become mainstream in the future.

Besides changes related to technological developments, social drives also play a role in fashioning English. The women's liberation and civil rights movements in America are examples of the phenomenon of altering acceptable discourse and focusing on political correctness. One example of the influence of the women's liberation movement is that a generation or so ago it was considered uncouth to use profanity in the presence of 'ladies.' Today, especially among the young, it is far less uncommon to hear such words used in mixed company by members of both genders.

The word *Ms.*, intentionally created to blur the distinction between a single or a married woman, is a relatively recent addition to the English language. Words such as *lady* are expected to be replaced by *woman*, and such words as *waiter* or *waitress* by the non-sexist designation *server*. Similar examples, such as the use of the term *Native Americans* for people in the States formerly called *Indians*, are associated with the civil rights movement. Note too the progression of what was and now has become a non-derogatory term for people of color in America. The expression *colored* (as in the National Association for the Advancement of Colored People (NAACP)—whose name has not been altered—was for a long time in vogue. At a later period, the word *negro* became preferred. Still later this was replaced by the term *Black*, which subsequently gave rise to the expression *African American*.

We saw earlier how English in the past was greatly modified by new populations entering and then influencing the language. Today, legal and illegal non-English speaking immigrants are settling in English speaking societies in great numbers. This is bound to play a role in the continuous development of the language. Factors such as borrowing words from other languages, when faced with the task of naming objects or happenings for which no English words exists, will no doubt continue. On October 4, 1957, when the then Soviet Union launched the first artificial satellite into orbit, American newspapers headlined this event with such phrases as "Russia launches Sputnik." Turning to an English dictionary at the time to discover the meaning of *Sputnik* was to no avail. Sputnik was the Russian word for artificial satellite for which at that time there was no English equivalent. The following year, new editions of American dictionaries included the word, which had overnight become part of the English language. From the above we see not only how quickly foreign words may enter the English language, but also that a dictionary is to language like a thermometer is to temperature. Just as a thermometer measures but does not create temperature, so a dictionary records and defines existing lexical items but does not produce them on its own.

Yet another constituent English language alteration is broadening existing word definitions to form fresh expressions. An example of this is the word *hot* which has recently been used by certain Hollywood celebrities to stress the likeability of something (as in "That outfit is hot."). The word *cool* has for some time been used in a similar capacity. The word *baby* may also be viewed as having entered this category. A generation or two ago, to call a youngster involved in a sport such as basketball *baby* would likely have been interpreted as an insult. Today the word is used to encourage (such as "Come on, baby") and to compliment or show appreciation (such as "That was a great play, baby.").

25

From the range of factors delineated above, it is clear that the English language through usage is in the process of change. With the acceleration of so much in our modern society, it may also be that these changes are occurring more rapidly than in the past. Until now, changes in spoken English were ahead of written change. With the advent and short-circuit use of such apparatuses as the computer and texting devices, this may not hold true in the future.

CHAPTER 4

Approaches Used in Teaching English to Non-English Speakers

In this section various methods which have been employed to teach English to non-English speakers will be identified and examined. Just as the English language is in a state of continuous change, so too are the processes used to teach it. Particular attention will be paid to a technique of instruction, the audio-lingual method (ALM), which made its appearance in America in 1942 and remained extremely popular for about three decades. Although some major programs such as the New York City-wide adult education programs employed it at least to some extent through the 1980s, numerous other programs began to abandon it in the late 1960s and early 1970s, when negative information about it was revealed. Until then ALM was considered in most language teaching circles to be a major breakthrough in English language development. Unlike other teaching methods, ALM was thought to be scientifically verified and, as such, became the flagship standard of English language instruction. About thirty years later, however, when the approach began to lose credibility, it began to decline in usage as a major teaching method. Ultimately, audiolingualism as a foundation course disappeared from the scene. The Audio-lingual method and its classroom application will be delineated in detail. Why such a popular teaching method fell into disfavor will also be examined. A brief description of other teaching methods is also included.

If one desires to travel from one destination to another, such as from New York City to Washington D.C., there are multiple ways to accomplish the task. One might travel by car, bus, train or plane. One might also choose to journey by motorcycle, bicycle, roller skates, horse, donkey-cart or even by foot. Although any of these choices might successfully achieve the objective, they are obviously not equally practical or efficient. The same may be said of English language teaching methodology. Since colonial times in America approaches to teaching English began to develop. However, since the early efforts were felt to be lacking, over the years other methods came into being. The process continues to the present day. A plethora of new methods emerged in the decade of the 1970s with the decline of the widely used ALM. New program development may essentially be viewed as an attempt to advance English language teaching by devising more efficient and effective methodology. Although the current segment will analyze the rise and decline of the Audio-lingual method, it is important to be acquainted with at least some of the techniques which preceded, paralleled and followed this approach. A listing of some past and present language teaching techniques was formulated by Dr. Jill Kerper Mora of San Diego State University.[14] Besides ALM, this list includes:

- The Grammar Translation approach
- The Direct approach
- Community Language Learning (CLL)
- The Silent Way
- The Total Physical Response approach
- The National Functional approach
- Communicative language teaching
- Task based learning

---

[14] Mora, J. K. (2010). Second language teaching methods: Principles and procedures. Retrieved from http://www.moramodules.com/ALMMethods.htm

To this list might be added:

- The literacy approach
- Suggestopedia
- Language immersion learning

As a result of the special attention given to the Audiolingual method or ALM (as an example of the decline of a highly praised ESL teaching method), the discussion of the methods itemized includes, where applicable, references to factors which may have influenced ALM's creation.

The retention of particular aspects of ALM in programs designed to replace it is also discussed.

The Literacy Approach

The literacy approach was an early method in the 1800s intended to teach the English language. The system emphasized written mastery in English in the style of imitating classical literature. Since, unlike audio-lingual instruction, it was not designed to assist students in using English in everyday matters, other techniques were soon sought

The Grammar Translation Approach

The grammar translation method soon replaced the literacy approach and became the major means to teach English as an additional language in the 1800s. This method required students to memorize rules of grammar and word lists for the purpose of accurately translating texts from English into their first language. The system was, however, seriously flawed. Lacking was emphasis on content, context, applying the material worked on to everyday situations, as well as emphasis on communication in English. Furthermore, critics maintained that frustration and tedium among students often set in as a result of their being required to memorize huge lists of unusable rules of grammar and vocabulary. They argued that the procedure did little to produce English speakers. However, despite these negative, components of the Grammar Translation approach were still reflected in later day programs. Certain elements of the system, at least to a small degree (such as emphasis on sentence structure and memorization of particular program items) were in fact incorporated into audio-lingual methodology.

The Direct Method

The direct method, also known as the natural method, evolved in Europe at the beginning of the twentieth century. Françoise Gouin and later Maximilian Berlitz are credited with developing and promoting this system which no doubt influenced the Audio-lingual method more than any other. It was based on the principle that to learn a new language it was necessary to imitate the way one learned their first language. Imitation was viewed as the natural way to learn a new language. Since it was maintained that children do not depend on a prior language to learn their first one, there was no need to employ their native language to learn another. In the direct method stress was placed primarily on learning vocabulary, but also on accurate pronunciation and on mastering the oral skills of the new language. Students were expected to communicate in the target language in all situations. One criticism of the system was that the level of communication expected could not realistically be attained in the classroom, which itself was an artificial setting. The method was, however, taken over by the Audio-lingual method with some modifications. For example, both methods advocated teaching a new language directly, without translations or explanations in the students' native language. The direct method tended to emphasize vocabulary learning through the use of objects, pictures and pantomime with students being left to determine grammar through imitation and trial and error as learning progressed. On the other hand, the Audio-lingual method stressed the use of drills, often referred to as "practice patterns," to help students gain proficiency in grammar. This differed from the direct method's primary emphasis of teaching vocabulary.

Community Language Learning

Not to be confused with Communicative language teaching, the Community Language Learning (CLL) approach was developed in the 1970s (as were other methods at the time) as an alternative to the decline of the Audio-lingual method. Greater emphasis was placed on the affective role in language learning, as opposed to relying on stimulus-response theory procedures, the key element of the Audio-lingual method. Although different from the Audiolingual method, CLL did borrow some elements from it. CLL, as did the audio-lingual program, looked beyond the realm of linguistics to the field of psychology for scientific validation. The CLL approach was influenced in its educational outlook by the noted psychologist Carl Rogers. Its approach was designed to make students feel at ease by removing the emotional blocks often associated with learning a new language. Other programs attempted to do the same. In CLL a counseling-learning structure was established, and the group taught was viewed as being in need of a particular kind of counseling. In this model the teacher played the role of a non-threatening counselor who allowed students to use their mother tongue, which their mentor then translated. No limits or boundaries were prescribed, and the learners' needs were primary. The system rested entirely on deductive learning. Critics of the system maintained that depending totally on deductive learning was detrimental. They argued too that instructors in the system were not sufficiently directive. In addition, they opined that without excellent translation ability on the part of the counselor, the method was unlikely to succeed.

Total Physical Response

The total physical response (TPR) method was originated by James Asher in the latter part of the 1970s. Although TPR agreed with the Audio-lingual method in certain respects, its major focus on learning through use of the kinesthetic sensory system resulted in it being quite different. TRP also believed that learning a new language is similar to how a child learns his first language, and that the listening skill must precede all others. Therefore, after listening, the learner is expected to demonstrate understanding by responding to a direction in a physical manner. The student in this method is never forced to speak but is instead given an individual readiness period before voluntarily beginning to vocalize in the new language. Critics of the system contend that it does not lend itself to teaching language well through intricate or complex structures. It has proven to be too cumbersome to do so. The TRP method has, however, not entirely disappeared. For example, instructors today who at times still use oral drills as in the audiolingual process give commands with structures of limited complexity.

The Notional-Functional Method, Communicative Language Teaching and Task Based Learning (TBL)

Since the communicative language technique and task based learning are in actuality refinements and, therefore, extensions of the notional-functional method, the three are discussed here collectively. In an attempt to deal with criticisms of the Audio-lingual method (ALM) in the late 1970s, long time proponents of ALM such as Mary Finochiaro sought new ways to remedy its shortfalls. Criticisms included boredom setting in with the over abundant use of choric drills, repetition of grammatical structures, and robot-like memorization and narration of monologues and dialogues. The context in which ALM material was presented was also questioned in terms of its relevance to students in their daily existence. In addition, although the

ALM dialogues presented to students revolved around motifs in everyday settings (such as ordering food in a restaurant, visiting the doctor, shopping for food or clothing, asking for directions, going to the post office, and so on), the transferability of such learning was judged to be limited outside such specific situations. In other words, a major impediment in the system was that students were unable to generalize by applying structures they had studied in class to new situations outside the classroom.

Early in the 1970s a new language teaching approach developed in Europe which caught the attention of some linguists in America. The approach centered on the meaning of language and on its execution by learners. At the beginning interested linguists in America played with the idea that parts of the new system might be integrated with ALM teaching to remedy the perceived difficulty ALM students faced in generalizing to new settings. The new approach was called notional-functional learning. Notions were depicted as place, expressions of time, amounts, beliefs, and so on. Functions included being critical, questioning matters, suggesting, asking for forgiveness, inviting and describing. Rather than a total method, a notional-functional syllabus organized according to what was termed "real communication" came into being (in contrast to an ALM curriculum based on progressive structures of grammar). For a period of time, this was the sole tool used for instruction. However, as the system continued to evolve it soon rejected the structuralist view prevalent in ALM that language was essentially a group of habits learned orally. The new view held that language was essentially social behavior. One's goal, therefore, was not to strive for perfect or near perfect language usage and pronunciation in predetermined settings, but rather to attain communication competence, even if imperfect, in all settings. With these refinements, the approach became known as communicative language teaching.

In communicative language teaching, essential dictums to generate language relevant to multiple situations was dependent on notional-functional syllabus material. The latter was designed to assess the meanings of speech forms and functional groups.

At a later time, studying the characteristics of interaction between students and instructors became part of the system. Methodology tended to become the primary focus of the system, more so than content which relied on notional-functional inventory. Critics pointed out that notions and functional content were undesirable in a learning situation because students were unlikely to possess the vocabulary and grammar (which was needed but not previously taught) to proceed in learning. Moreover, no all-inclusive itemization of notions and functions was available, nor could such an inventory realistically be produced.

What emerged too from notional-functional communicative learning was the task based learning approach. Although this approach brings to mind the total physical response method in the sense that the completion of a task was used both as a means to organize instruction as well as to assess learning, there was a significant difference. Task based learning students, when given a task, were expected to use spoken English to complete it. In this process, once a task was determined, the teacher would convey some vocabulary and phrases to prepare students to perform it. Students would then complete the task using the limited vocabulary and phrases by the teacher had introduced at the start, with any additional English vocabulary the students might possess. However, there was only minimal correction of verbal errors that occurred during the process. Although verbal expression was encouraged, the primary concern of the process was on understanding a language in order to learn it. Verbal production was thus relegated to a secondary position.

From the standpoint of critics, not enough language points are generally taught in advance of students being expected to undertake the task. They contend that more emphasis is needed on language production. There is no place in the program, for example, for teaching meaningful grammar. The teacher's input is viewed as choppy bits of language without controlled practice which, they feel, lessens the effectiveness of the approach. In addition, what the teacher conveys is often arbitrary and, therefore, frequently irrelevant to student needs. Critics also raise questions pertaining to the overall premise of the procedure—that language is derived from motor activity.

The Silent Way

Caleb Gattegno (1911-1988), creator of the silent way, was undeniably a genius who perceived language learning in a unique way. The silent way, another program which emerged in the 1970s, was distinctive in the sense that it was totally unrelated to any of the other language systems. In the silent way, the learner was urged to discover rather than memorize and repeat. The teacher in this system was mostly silent so that the students could produce the language they learned on their own.

The teacher's role was to observe and at critical times to model or present new items such as vocabulary, pronunciation, structural patterns and rules of grammar, but only once. Learners were then tasked with incorporating the new information into their efforts and continuing to learn on their own through the process of induction. At periodic times, when the teacher tested students, the mode of silence was abandoned. Physical objects to help facilitate learning consisted of color coded word charts (in which each phoneme or sound in a language which differentiates between meanings such as his and hiss) were used, as were Cuisenaire rods (small colored wooden blocks of different sizes). These items became associated with the system and are usually referred to in discussions about it.

The Silent Way then was an effort to encourage students to work as a group to gain knowledge of a new language while the teacher served strictly as a guide. It was based on the principle that discovery on its own resulted in far greater retention than when information was attained without struggle, through the lectures of an instructor. According to Gattegno, teaching in this method was "as it should be, subordinated to learning." This system, like all others, had no lack of critics. It was maintained that the method could only be practiced in small classes.

Although small size is desirable in almost all language teaching, it is not usually practical. Critics contended further that certain components of English which were challenging to the students should be directly conveyed by the teacher. They also maintained that greater overall teacher involvement in the lessons was needed.

Suggestopedia

Suggestopedia, created by Bulgarian psychologist George Lozanov, made its debut in the late 1970s. Although it was distinctively different from community language learning, both programs shared the outlook that a relaxed, anxiety free atmosphere was required for effective language learning to flourish, and the concept that students' fears of being unable to learn and process new language information created mental blocks. Accordingly, for new language to be acquired, it was essential that such psychological barriers be removed. To create the levels of concentration needed, comfortable seating was arranged in a dimly lit atmosphere, and baroque music was played. The aim was that these features would relax the students so they could retain what was taught. In this system the instructor is given full control and may at times serve somewhat like a hypnotist to make students suggestive to learning. Critics of the technique question the premise that students are so fearful of learning a new language that they enter the program with mental or psychological barriers. They also point to the lack of any student input in the learning and to the dominant role played by the instructor.

Language Immersion

As new programs emerged to fill the gap left by the decline of ALM, language immersion was explored. In its purest form, language immersion learning may be understood best by picturing a person who decides to live in a foreign country or environment where no one speaks their native tongue in order to learn the language of the community. As they attempt to function among the inhabitants, they have no choice but to work on picking up the language. For adults arriving in the U.S.A. a formal language immersion program would be difficult to structure. Newly arriving immigrants generally seek to settle near others like themselves who have arrived earlier and can communicate with them in their native language. As a result, the need of new arrivals to learn English is not as pressing as that of someone in a situation where no one can communicate with them in their native language.

Somewhat modified English immersion programs, which were not meant to be adult orientated, have been established for young non-English speaking students in some venues. In such situations the students are placed in an environment where they must strive to use English. In one such locality, students enrolled in a bilingual English immersion program are exposed to English in some form the entire school day. They are instructed at least partially in English in all school subjects, such as social studies, science, mathematics, and so on. A formula is generally established in this type of program, with instruction in the early grades consisting of forty percent of English and sixty percent in the student's native language, for example. In the upper grades the percentages are usually reversed with more instructional time (namely a ratio of 60/40 percent) devoted to English. Eventually, English alone is expected to be used.

Some immersion programs are criticized because outside the classroom students revert to almost exclusive use of their native language. In other instances, it is argued that fluency but not accuracy of usage in English is the end result. Still others contend that how effectively English is used outside the school is simply unknown.

CHAPTER 5

The Audiolingual Method

At the start of World War II the United States government became concerned with such matters as building Western hemisphere solidarity through English language teaching among other things. Under President Franklin Roosevelt's Good Neighbor policy selective Latin American professionals and students were given the opportunity to learn English. At about the same time, the US government was concerned with identifying military personnel who were fluent in foreign languages such as German, Italian, French, Chinese and Japanese. Such personnel were needed to serve as translators, code breakers and interpreters. It was soon discovered, however, that there was a shortage of military personnel who were proficient in the languages sought. If a method could be found for teams of military staff to be taught a foreign language in a relatively short period of time, and for others to be able to apply the method to teaching English without being proficient in the students' native language, the problem of personnel shortage would be resolved. Fortunately, research was being conducted at the University of Michigan which had the potential to develop such a program.

The English Language Institute (ELI) of the University of Michigan was founded in 1941 as an experimental endeavor by Dr. Charles Fries, who received a $3000 grant from the Rockefeller Foundation. ELI focused both on research and on the teaching of English to non-English speakers. As a result of the military need which existed for an effective language teaching method, the United States State Department under the 1942 army specialized training program (ASTP) turned to the institute and soon supported it. The institute's mission then became to devise cultural programs but, more importantly, to develop a first rate language teaching method which would accelerate foreign language learning and also be used by monolingual English instructors to teach English to Latin Americans. The University of Michigan's ELI was the first such facility to be established in the U.S.A. However, already by 1943, as a result of government funding, more than 50 American universities were functioning with similar language centers.

Charles Fries, the Michigan Institute's director, in an effort to meet the language method challenge, promoted the fundamentals of structural linguistics. This was a new approach, an American one, which differed from European language teaching. In Fries's system, comparisons between English and other languages were emphasized to assist foreign language learning. Much use was made of contrastive analysis, with the view that a major block to learning a foreign language was unfamiliarity with its structural system. The work at the institute resulted in a method which stressed listening or aural training first, followed by speaking and then reading and writing. Oral repetition drills rather than the use of written exercises were employed to teach grammatical patterns. Vocabulary learning was primarily limited to those words needed for drill repetition. Working closely with Fries was Robert Lado, who became ELI's director after Fries retired. Both men were influenced by the work of the American linguist Leonard Bloomfeld. In the early 1900s Bloomfeld had produced a theoretical description of indigenous languages spoken in the USA. In conducting his research, he had to rely almost solely on observation. For that reason his work focused primarily on the oral aspect of language. Bloomfeld's oral emphasis influenced Fries to conclude that language was essentially speech. This meant that language is speech first and foremost, and that writing is only the recording of what is spoken. Speech in other words is considered more basic than writing to language.

The views of those at the English Language Institute were also influenced by the outlook of the noted behavioral psychologist B. F. Skinner. Skinner maintained that language, like behavior, was learned through a stimulus-response mechanism which required repetition and reinforcement. Incorporating this outlook, Fries developed an oral-habit method of language teaching. It became the very first to claim legitimacy, not only through linguistic theory but also through behaviorist psychological theory. Links to both these fields no doubt contributed to the method's popularity as well as to its staying power of several decades.

The learning system that emerged from the work of Fries's institute was a blend of concepts derived from structural linguistics, contrastive analysis, aural-oral techniques and behaviorist psychology. At its inception, because of the role played by The United States army in commissioning the University of Michigan to develop its program, the approach was termed 'the Army method.' As time moved on, other names were used, such as the oral approach. Later such terms as the structural approach and the applied linguistics method were added. In addition, because the method called for students to imitate, mimic and memorize dialogues, the title Mim-Mem method came into being. Ultimately, as the approach gained wider acceptance, it was designated the Audiolingual method (ALM), or more simply, Audiolingualism.

The Audiolingual method incorporated many of the features of an earlier program, the direct method. ALM stressed listening before speaking, speaking before reading and reading before writing. It was also identified with the view that a student's mother tongue was not to be used by either the student or the classroom instructor. In its early and purest form, both these principles were firmly adhered to. In time, however, certain modifications of the technique were suggested by its practitioners and by its leader, Robert Lado. These changes were incorporated into the method. Some of these adjustments were thought to conflict with the method's fundamental philosophy. Through usage, however, it was found that concessions such as using the student's native language at times, and not insisting strictly on speaking before reading enhanced the program's effectiveness. Despite criticism that allowing such changes would diminish the basic rationale upon which Audiolingualism was based, the program's overall outlook and philosophy essentially remained intact.

Credit must be given to those who believed in the program's fundamental view, yet did not hesitate to experiment and, when necessary, step outside its boundaries to improve learning. In February 1980, for example, Robert Lado addressed a group of Title VI Adult Education Teachers in New York City at a conference sponsored by the Federation of Jewish Philanthropies. At that meeting he demonstrated and advocated using a technique for the memorization of dialogues. He acknowledged that the technique tended to deviate from the standard practice of speaking before reading but pointed out his research indicated that literate ESOL students master dialogues more quickly when the technique in question is employed. In the suggested process, students were asked to listen to the teacher read a dialogue from the chalkboard as the teacher pointed to each word. The students were then asked to read the dialogue as a group, while the teacher continued to point to the words as they were stated. After the group had read the dialogue several times, the teacher would erase several key words. The students were then again requested to read the dialogue as though no erasures had been made. The process of erasing words would continue after every group reading until there were no longer any words left on the board. The students by this time had memorized the dialogue and could be called upon for individual rote recitations.

Despite the creativity and flexibility displayed by ALM advocates, events transpired which resulted in the continuously dwindling use of ALM as the foundation of a course. The reasons for the decline of this popular program will be explored later. At this point, however, it is of interest to learn more about how the program functioned. What follows, therefore, is a description of the philosophy and approach that those taught to employ the audiolingual technique were presented with. The description includes the method's later modifications.

A. The Audiolingual Method or ALM Philosophy on Language Acquisition

In order to understand what skills are involved in using language, one should first understand the ALM view of language and of language acquisition.

What is language? From the standpoint of ALM, language is something we hear. However, not everything we hear is language. Noise, for example, is not language because it has no meaningful order or pattern. One is unable to tell in advance what sound will be next if one is listening to noise. Language, on the other hand, is organized into meaningful patterns and structures (how the sounds in a language are put together). Those help us to differentiate language from plain sound.

If students are unfamiliar with a particular language, they are also unfamiliar with that language's pattern and structure. For this reason, it may at first sound like noise when they hear it. This, of course, is not true for the speakers of that language. In order to learn a new language, we must learn which sounds are used in it, how these sounds are structured and the meaning of these structures. The most important thing is for the learner to know what the sounds and structures of the language being learned mean. Formally learning the rules of the language one is trying to master may be helpful, but it is not essential for understanding and speaking it. Children, for example, are brought up to understand and speak at least one language, but are generally unaware of why they say things as they do.

When we talk about understanding and speaking a language we talk about developing the learner's receptive (listening) and productive (speaking) skills. Since the language most Americans use in everyday matters is informal, it is informal English speech that should be taught to non-English speakers. It furthermore should be taught in the natural way we speak. Pronouncing words extra carefully or attempting to read them letter by letter will only interfere with the learning process.

For this reason, it is important that students hear and attempt to say words and structures they are learning accurately before being exposed to them in print. Reading and writing do not involve the same interactions as communicating orally. (For example, in speaking one may speak, pause, listen and then speak again). To gain the latter skills, a great deal of time must be spent in speaking orally. Oral reading is not a substitute for this. It is not the same as verbally communicating. Words and structures to teach oral communication should be ones that are used naturally. Although a dictionary will probably be useful to new speakers, it will not teach them how to use certain words.

B. The ALM View on Presenting the Basic Language Skills

Unless a person can understand and speak a language, he obviously does not know it very well. Understanding language without being able to converse in it is limiting. Likewise, people who can only handle the graphic (reading and writing) aspect of a language are also limited in terms of full communication. Reading and writing should be taught only after one has learned to hear and imitate sounds. Once students are somewhat familiar with the sounds of the new language they are learning, they can be shown how these are represented graphically. The general rule of thumb in teaching a student a new language is, therefore, as follows:

- Listening before speaking
- Speaking before reading
- Reading before writing

Because listening, speaking, reading and writing are separate skills, knowing one does not necessarily mean the learner has mastered the others. Students may be able to do well on a written test and yet not be able to understand what is said to them or be able to speak in the language studied. Of course, the implication should not be drawn from the above that students should be stopped from saying anything until they have learned to understand everything they hear, or stopped from writing until they become extremely fluent speakers. Listening, speaking, reading and writing go together, and each skill should be used to reinforce the others. The sequence of how such reinforcement takes place, however, is what is primary. If the listening, speaking, reading and writing sequence is not followed, it will probably take longer for a new learner to master the language. If non-English speakers, for example, are initially represented with new English material in graphic form, they will undoubtedly use sounds for the letters that they are familiar with in their own language. As mentioned previously, if Hispanic students are presented with the word *ship*, they are more likely than not to read it as *sheep*. This is because the /i/ in Spanish is pronounced as an *ee* sound. If the word is mastered orally first, the wrong sound is less likely to be reinforced by the native language.

C. ALM Outlook on Teaching a New Language

Students must learn to use the structure of the new language they are learning. Practice in using these structures is the best way to learn them. The teacher should model the new structure first and encourage the student to say it soon afterwards. Corrections should be made accordingly. It is generally considered better not to encourage the student to ask questions in their native language about what is being taught. Such interactions may slow down rather than enhance the process of the student speaking English. Instead of translating, a teacher should attempt to use pictures, objects and gestures to convey meaning of new structures. This may take more time, but it is ultimately more helpful to the student. However, since it is particularly important that students thoroughly understand what they are attempting to say (when repeating a structure after the teacher models it), it is better for the teacher to use the students' native language to give explanations when they are unable to understand otherwise. This way, students need not repeat structures that are meaningless to them.

The advantage of teachers who do not have the ability to make explanations in the native language of their students (because of unfamiliarity with their language) is, of course, that they are unlikely to become dependent on a translation approach. The more students use a new language, the quicker they will become proficient at it. However, before students can be expected to speak a new language freely, they must be taught how to express themselves in it. Dialogues and practice patterns or drills are a major part of audiolingual instruction. Dialogues are presented for students to understand the context in which the structures they are being taught may be employed. Practice patterns serve as a reinforcement device and are a distinguishable characteristic of the audiolingual method.

D. ALM Suggestions on Working with Students

Student expectations should be kept in mind when attempting to help them learn English. If teachers fail to deal with the expectations of students, there is the likelihood that they will resist any attempts the instructor makes to teach them. For example, a student may believe that the most effective way to learn English is by reading and writing and not by emphasizing oral communication. As was pointed out earlier, since reading and writing should be used to reinforce oral language skills, it is possible to proceed with the listening, speaking, reading and writing sequence and still satisfy the student.

It is not possible to anticipate every problem that arises, since they vary from individual to individual. Solutions to problems will often have to be worked out creatively. In the end, students should feel that their expectations are being met, but effective up-to-date methodology should not be compromised. Learning to function in the fashion described above is part of the reason teaching is considered an art. In general, once the teacher gains the trust of the students, it will be easier for them to accept the methodology. Seeing where their goals fit into the goals the instructor has for the group is important. As students realize they are making progress, they will become more trusting and more willing to accept the methodology.

It is important in language teaching that the students and teacher be able to both see and hear each other. Students must, of course, hear sounds before they can be expected to repeat them. Observing someone producing the sound is also helpful. The teacher serves as a model for students by pronouncing sounds which they then attempt to imitate. Students should sit in a position where they are able to see and hear the teacher pronounce the sounds they are trying to learn.

When structures which are associated with physical activities are taught, it is suggested that students carry out the physical activities being spoken about where possible. This will help students to associate actions with sounds more clearly and will probably also help them to retain new learning for a longer time period. For example, if a student says they are giving their book to someone, they should be handing the book over to a neighbor. After having completed this task, they might be asked what they did. It is particularly important at the beginning for students to carry out what they say they are doing. This is a form of reinforcement which helps tie reality to the spoken word. Language learning involves the use of a number of senses. It involves mental as well as physical activities. The more senses used, the more effective the learning will be. The use of actual objects while assisting students in learning English should be incorporated into the teaching. A student should handle such objects as a pen and a pencil as he is learning their names. When you want a student to say, "This is a wallet," it is best that they hold such an object. The environment of the classroom can also be used. The teacher can ask about the number of chairs in the room, whether a particular window is open or closed, whether lights are on or off, and so on. Important classroom events of the day can also be brought into the picture. The basic idea is to keep the language learning as real and in turn as relevant as possible.

Students should be given practice in the various aspects of oral language. Rather than responding only to the teacher, they should be given the opportunity to initiate discussion and practice in generating their own sentences. This comes about once students get involved with the teacher in conversations or work in pairs or in small groups with their fellow students. During such activities they should be encouraged to ask questions and make statements, besides responding to the teacher's directions and questions.

E. Language Skills for Presentation to ALM Students on Different Levels

ESOL: Examples of Abilities and Needs in the Skills Areas

	LISTENING	SPEAKING
Beginners	▪ Very little or no comprehension ▪ Needs work in hearing phonetic differences ▪ Needs to become accustomed to the *music* of English (stress, rhythm, intonation) ▪ Needs to be exposed to basic English structures and vocabulary	▪ Very limited ability ▪ Generally confined to responding in broken sentences or one syllable words ▪ Heavy accent needs correction ▪ Needs to repeat simple sentences modeled by English speakers with correct *music* ▪ Needs help in forming substitute sentences ▪ Needs exposure to a variety of structures sand vocabulary items

Intermediate	■ Fair comprehension and less difficulty in hearing phonemic differences and English *music* ■ Needs to continue to tune in to English conversations, speeches, news reports, to distinguish the fine points of how the language is spoken	■ Can produce many structures with a variety of lexical items ■ Speaks less haltingly and is more easily understood ■ Sound system of English is still not mastered
	■ May still need work in hearing certain phonemic differences, understanding word order meaning of verb tenses ■ Should be able to read with comprehension what is learned orally	■ Needs work with English word order, perfection of sounds nonexistent in own language, production of simple sentences, application of English grammatical forms to new vocabulary
	READING	**WRITING**
Beginners	■ Is unable to read and may not know the names and sounds of the letters of the alphabet ■ Should be taught consonant and vowel sounds, sight recognition of own name and other words frequently used orally ■ Should be taught punctuation	■ Very limited: may confuse manuscript and cursive forms ■ Should learn to write name ■ Should be taught to form capital and small letters and apply correctly

Intermediate	<ul><li>Can read simple sentences and decode words which follow standard rules</li><li>Should be taught to find meanings of words in dictionary and ascertain meaning from context</li><li>Should be taught to decode exceptions</li><li>Should understand meaning of verb tenses</li><li>Should be able to read with comprehension what is learned orally</li></ul>	<ul><li>Still limited</li><li>Needs to learn to copy sentences with proper punctuation</li><li>Lear to fill in basic forms</li><li>Learn to answer simple questions in writing</li><li>Should be taught to take some dictation</li><li>Should be taught to write friendly and business letters</li></ul>
Advanced	<ul><li>Can read daily newspaper with comprehension</li><li>Should learn to paraphrase, identify unusual words, foreign words, summarize, read between the lines</li><li>Should be familiar with more advanced dictionary skills; use of encyclopedia, Dewey Decimal System, map and globe skills</li></ul>	<ul><li>Can handle but still somewhat faulty</li></ul> Teach to:<ul><li>Write more freely</li><li>Write stories and compositions</li><li>Write summaries</li></ul>

F. ALM Suggestions for Planning a Sound ESL Lesson

Contents of a Good ESL Lesson

1. Some small talk should be included.
2. The lesson may begin with either the entire group or with small groups. The teacher should attempt to include

everyone in the group activities and also allot time for individualization.

3. The lesson should include activities which involve the following:

- Review of previous learning
- New learning
- Sound system emphasis (rhythm, stress, intonation, pronunciation)
- Practice patterns (choral, small group, individual, chain, backward buildup, transformation, substitution)
- Vocabulary building (should include vocabulary previously learned and the introduction of new vocabulary through familiar structures, using props, pictures or actual objects)
- Sentence structure (review of previously learned structures followed by the gradual introduction of new ones). Many variations are desirable. Reinforcement must be stressed and includes reading and writing. Final evaluation involves the use of the structures by the students in meaningful situations.

G. ALM Suggestions for the Use of Practice Patterns

While language may have formal rules, learning these will not necessarily help one to speak a new language adequately. Speakers have to develop habits of using their voice in new ways, quickly and correctly; of adding inflections, prefixes and suffixes to words; of putting words in order and combinations required by English; and of using appropriate language in various communication situations. Listeners must learn to recognize and react to the oral signals they hear in any message. It is only through practice that the competence to understand and transmit the message can be gained. Practice patterns should follow items presented in oral communication situations. There are numerous variations of such patterns, several of which are given in this section. Before attempting to perform oral practice, the following should be kept in mind.

- The words spoken in the practice pattern should be authentic or those that a native speaker uses. They should make sense and be relevant to the students' interests and lives.
- Words spoken should relate to structures or to the vocabulary area. Consequently, communication will come more quickly, and a real conversation will develop.
- Other patterns should be practiced—in mini-situations. For example: Thank you. Be careful. How are you? Don't worry. I will.
- The substitution practice pattern should usually be presented after the choric drill so students gain the habit of arranging words in correct positions.
- In the practice pattern immediately after the first presentation the change should be minimal, or only one change should be made.
- The teacher should give students several examples and serve as a model calling upon students to respond.
- Some of the practice patterns are more appropriate for practicing a particular item than others. For example, when teaching adjectives, the expansion, substitution and transformation practice pattern would be most effective. Only the practice pattern most appropriate for teaching an item should be used.
- The teacher should lead the practice pattern as a conductor leads an orchestra. The teacher should use both hand signals and cue words.

Samples of Some ALM Practice Patterns (Drills)

The Choric Practice Pattern

A Choric Practice Pattern for Beginners: the imitation of spoken material by an entire class or by a group speaking together.

Student one to student two:

1. Hello!
2. Good morning!

1. I'm John Smith
2. Are you Bill Jones?
1. Yes, I am.

1. How are you?
2. Fine, thanks.

A More Advanced Choric Practice Pattern

First the teacher explains:

Stan grew up and lives in California. He recently visited New York City for the first time. He stayed there for several days. He and his friend Bob are talking about New York City.

Practice Pattern

Bob: Did you like New York City?
Stan: Yes, I did. I liked it very much. It's an exciting city.
Bob: How long were you there?
Stan: I stayed there ten days. It's expensive. I didn't have enough money to stay any longer.
Bob: I understand. I visited New York City two years ago before my Aunt Betty moved to Israel.
Stan: That's interesting. Did you stay at your aunt's home?
Bob: Yes, I did. I had to. A hotel would have been too expensive.

Question and Answer Practice

At a later point students can be asked questions about the dialogue to give them practice in answering questions. For example, questions such as the following might be asked:

Where does Stan live?
Did Stan go to New York City to live there?
Did Stan stay in New York City for several weeks? Did he stay for a few days?
Did Stan like New York City?
Was Bob in New York City last year? When was Bob in New York City?
Where did Bob stay when he visited New York City?
What do Stan and Bob think about costs in New York City?

Advantages of the Choric Practice Pattern

1. Students are not embarrassed by being called on individually.
2. They gain the opportunity to master the structure through group practice.
3. Students have a chance for self-correction in a nonthreatening situation.

Substitution Practice Pattern

Substitution practice pattern: Replacement of a word in a structure with another word.
Students must recall what is said in each sentence in order to form the new sentence.

Procedure:

Teacher	Student
I have a red pencil.	I have a red pencil.
green	I have a green pencil.
He	He has a green pencil.
pen	He has a green pen.
Mr. Jones	Mr. Jones has a green pen.
four	Mr. Jones has four green pens.
They	They have four green pens.
need	They need four green pens.

Note: Other words can also be used.

Transformation Practice Pattern

Transformation: The conversion of a structure to a different form.

Example: Change affirmative statement to negative statement such as: "It's a nice day" to "It's not a nice day."

Procedure: The instructor will give the model sentence and say, for example, "Now we're going to make questions from these sentences." Say, "She has a pencil." The student(s) will say, "Does she have a pencil?"

Backward Build-Up Practice Pattern

Backward Build-Up: The teaching technique whereby long sentences are divided and reconstructed from the end into small meaningful segments for ease in repetition.

Example: Here is the procedure for learning a sentence from the end. Let us take, "She's going to sleep now."

Procedure:
1. Say the entire sentence many times.
2. Say "now." Class repeats "now."
3. Say "sleep." Class repeats "sleep."
4. Say "sleep now." Class repeats "sleep now."
5. Say "going to." Class repeats "going to."
6. Say "going to sleep now." Class repeats "going to sleep now."
7. Say "She's going to sleep now." Class repeats "She's going to sleep now."

Very often, particularly when a long sentence is uttered which a student is directed to repeat, the first part is recalled but not the last. By beginning at the end and working backwards in small segments, a student is usually able to produce the entire sentence quickly.

An example of this is when an English speaking child or adult who is unfamiliar with the tongue twister, "Peter Piper picked a peck of pickled peppers" is asked to repeat it. After saying, "Peter Piper" or "Peter Piper picked," they are likely to be lost. However, by using the backward build-up technique, they can generally be taught to master this twister perfectly. The drill might be employed as follows:

The teacher asks the student to say: "pickled peppers."

The student repeats: "pickled peppers."

Teacher: "a peck of pickled peppers"

Student: "a peck of pickled peppers"

Teacher: "picked a peck of pickled peppers"

Student: "picked a peck of pickled peppers"

Teacher: "Peter Piper picked a peck of pickled peppers."

Student: "Peter Piper picked a peck of pickled peppers."

The Chain Drill

The teacher begins a chain drill by asking an individual student a question. The student responds with a single answer, or with a choice of several answers. The student then asks the same question of the student sitting beside him. This continues in a chain fashion until all students have had the opportunity both to respond and to ask their neighbor the question.

Example of a chain drill

Question: Do you do your own cooking?

Possible Responses:

Yes, I do. I'm a good cook.

No, I don't. My wife (husband) cooks for me (us).
Sometimes I do, but sometimes I eat at my sister's house.
                                        (a friend's house)
                                        (a restaurant)

The use of the chain drill involves controlled communication and allows the teacher to check on each student's verbal response.

The Expansion Drill

An expansion drill is designed to help students produce longer sentences and be comfortable in reciting them.

Examples of an Expansion Drill

Example 1

The teacher asks the question: "What is it like in the summer?"

The student at first is encouraged to respond with one characteristic of summer such as:

"It is sunny in the summer."

The teacher directs the student to retain the sentence but to insert the word **very** in a proper slot. The sentence then becomes:

"It is **very** sunny in the summer."

Additional directions are given, one or two words at a time, to make the sentence grow. This continues until the sentence is stretched or expanded far beyond what it was originally.

Example 1:

It is very sunny and hot in the summer.

It is very sunny, hot and humid in the summer.

It is very sunny, very hot and very humid in the summer.

Example 2

Teacher:"Was yesterday Sunday?"

Student:"Yes, yesterday was Sunday."

Teacher:"Add the words, 'and today is Monday.'"

Student:"Yes, yesterday was Sunday and today is Monday."

Teacher:"Add the words, 'which is the beginning of the work week.'"

Student:"Yes, yesterday was Sunday, and today is Monday, which is the beginning of the work week."

H. ALM Suggestion for Introducing New Vocabulary

New vocabulary should be introduced through structures which are already familiar to students. After relevant vocabulary situations are identified, vocabulary necessary to such situations can be developed, then taught to the students. Relevant vocabulary situations for adults might include the following:

- Ordering meals in a restaurant
- Asking for street directions
- Calling the fire or police department
- Getting an apartment
- Going for a job interview
- Shopping in a particular store (drugstore, fruit and vegetable store, grocery)
- Making a doctor's appointment

A sample vocabulary list for ordering meals is as follows:

Vocabulary List

Ordering Meals

a la carte	jelly	tax
appetizer	juice	tax
		tea
bag	ketchup	teaspoon
beer	knife	thirsty
beverage (drink)		tip
bib	lemon	to-go

bowl	lunch	toast
bread		toothpick
breakfast	main course	tray
butter	manager	
	margarine	vegetable
cafeteria	meal	
cashier	menu	water
cereal (hot/cold)	milk	waiter
change	muffin	waitress
charge	mustard	wine
check		water
chicken	napkin	
clean		
coffee (black)	order	
complete dinner		
container	pepper	
counter	pizza	
crackers	plate	
cream	potatoes	
credit card		
delicious	reservation	
desert	restaurant	
dine	rest room	
diner	salad	
dinner	salt	
dirty	sandwich	
donuts	saucer	
	sauerkraut	
eat	sausage	
eggs	soup	
entrée	spicy	
	spoon	
fish	steak	
fork	sticky	
	straw	

glass	sugar	
	spicy	
hamburger (well done—rare)		
high chair	table	
hot chocolate	table for two	
hot dog	tablespoon	
hungry	tablecloth	
	take out	
ice cubes	tasty	

I. ALM Criteria for Evaluating Commercial ESOL Materials for Adults

- Is the material appropriate for adults?
- Is it adult oriented?
- Is it life or experience related?
- Does it meet the needs, the interests or the motivation of the group?
- Are the dialogues authentic, logical, relevant?
- Does the material encourage communication with English speakers?
- Does it develop awareness of some insights into the culture of English speaking people?

Instructional Appropriateness

- Are the dialogues short?
- It is easier to understand the meaning of short dialogues.
- Short dialogues are easier to memorize (a manageable amount of material).
- Does the material contain high frequency sentence structures and vocabulary?
- Does the material provide for listening opportunities?
- Is the material sequentially and systematically developed?

- **Example:** Is new vocabulary introduced through familiar vocabulary?
- Are new structures introduced through familiar vocabulary?
- **Example:** Are substitution practice patterns introduced prior to more complex transformation practices?
- **Example:** Are old structures reviewed before new ones are introduced, or is the introduction of new structures gradual?
- Are variations of structures and vocabulary given?
- **Example:** Are alternative words given in context?
- Is a variety of practice patterns presented or suggested? (choral, group, individual, substitution)
- Is evaluation of student progress considered by the writers of the material?
- Are evaluation measures suggested?
- Does the material lend itself to reinforcement and review of learning?
- **Example:** Through special reading exercises?
- **Example:** Through special writing exercises?
- Does the material contain useful and clear pictures or illustrations?
- Is the price and format of the material satisfactory? (shape, size, type of paper, binding, and so on)

J. Identifying Speaking Errors of Advanced ESOL Students

Below are some speaking errors made by an advanced ESL Russian student. Lessons can be developed that are based on errors made by advanced ESL students in the expressions they use in free conversation.

"You must be sure all what Solzhenitsyn writes is true."

"This is no good method."

"Two hundred thousand go to this country."

"Was bad climate."

"But was a sick area."

"Many people was go back."

"After second war many people go back."

"Impossible other newspaper."

A contrastive analysis of English compared to a student's mother tongue was an additional tool ALM ESOL teachers often found helpful. Errors such as those made by the Russian student might be anticipated and prepared for by the teacher through such an analysis. The following contrasts the English and Russian languages.

Contrastive Analysis Usage

A Contrastive Analysis of the English and Russian Languages

ENGLISH	RUSSIAN
The auxiliary *will*: "I will go with you."	Both auxiliaries and inflections are used, often leading to confusion in English.
The use of the word *it* to begin a sentence as in: "It is Saturday."	*It* is omitted in Russian because impersonal pronouns are not used. The sentence in question is often incorrectly spoken as: "Is Saturday."
The negative imperative *don't* as in: "Don't go!"	*Don't* might be replaced by a Russian speaker with *no*. the sentence formed might, therefore, be: "No go!"
The continuous present as in: "I am talking now."	The continuous present form is nonexistent in Russian. It may be substituted by the simple present as in: "I now talk."

The use of *that* and the consistency of tense in the clauses of a sentence as in: "She stated that she observed the Sabbath."	In Russian *that* is always followed by the present. The sentence might therefore be constructed as: "She stated that she observes (or is observing) the Sabbath."
Contractions such as: *he's, they're, I'll*	Contractions such as these do not exist in Russian.
The auxiliary *have* in the present perfect: "I have always gone to the synagogue on the Sabbath."	The simple present is likely to be substituted to form: "I always go to the synagogue on the Sabbath."
The definite article *the* and the indefinite article *a* as in: "The boy is wearing a hat."	No such articles exist in Russian. The sentence might be constructed as: "Boy wearing hat."
Use of possessive adjectives when referring to clothing or parts of the body as in: "My head aches."	Although no definite article exists in Russian, the definite article *the* is often substituted for a possessive adjective by Russian speakers. The sentence may, therefore, be constructed as: "The head aches."
Questions with *do, did, does* as in: "Does he work nights?"	Auxiliaries such as *do, did,* and *does* do not exist in Russian. The sentence may, therefore, be constructed as: "He work(s) nights? Or "Nights works he?"
Use of the verb *be* to express a condition such as: "I am lonely."	*To be* or *to have* may be substituted to form: "I lonely" or "I have lonely."
Use of the verb *be* when referring to age as in: "I'm forty-two."	The structures may simply take the form of "Me forty-two." The word *have* may be substituted as in: "I have forty-two (years)."

Adverbs, when coming prior to a reference to where or when such as: "He studies very hard every night."	Russian speakers have a tendency to reverse this form as in: "He studies every night very hard."
English compound verbs such as in: "I go down to get the paper every afternoon."	No compound verbs exist in Russian.
The /h/ sound as in *have*	"Ch" as in *Chanukah* or /g/ as in *go* is often substituted for /h/. *Had* may, therefore, be pronounced as "Chad" or "gad."
The /th/ sound	De or Ze is often substituted for /th/.
The /er/ sound as in tower	The /er/ sound does not exist in Russian. *Tower* may, therefore, be pronounced *tow*.

Minimal Pairs

ALM concern with proper English pronunciation has led to the development of identifying particular phonetic sounds in English which a student's native language may not contain. Or if existent, they may have no bearing on word meanings and are, therefore, ignored. An example of the latter phenomenon as pointed out in the section on Phonemes and Allophones is the sound of the letter /p/ in English. The sound of this letter is different when spoken in the words *pie* and *lip*.

The /p/ pronunciation is significantly stronger in the word *lip*, to the point that a lit candle might be blown out, if held close to the mouth of the speaker enunciating the sound. On the other hand, the /p/ in the word pie is a softer sound, which would not affect a candle flame. Most native English speakers are unaware of such differences because word meaning in English are not altered by them. However, to reiterate, the same letter's sounds in another language may in fact make a difference in the meaning of particular words.

As discussed in the Phonemes and Allophones section, students may substitute a sound they are familiar with in their native language for the correct English one, if the sound does not exist in that language. Such students might actually not even hear the English sound because it does not exist for them. Therefore, before attempting to get students to pronounce a sound, it is wise to determine whether in fact they hear it. There are techniques to ascertain this. For example, a student can be shown a way to signal whether two items are the same or different. The teacher might hold up two identical pencils and state that they are *the same*. Then, holding up a pencil and a book, they could state that the items are *different*. After several such displays, the teacher might indicate that holding up one finger signals *same*, while two fingers indicate *different*. The teacher would then proceed to pronounce such minimal pair words as *sheep-sheep* and later *sheep-ship* while at the same time viewing the students' held up fingers. In this way it can be ascertained which students hear the sound differences and which do not recognize them.

Once students can distinguish between sounds (such as a native Spanish speaker who now hears the difference but still substitutes the /i/ sound as in the word *sheep* for the short /i/ sound in the word *ship*), minimal pair practice can be used to help pronounce the short /i/ sound correctly. In addition, it may be necessary to demonstrate where the tongue is placed in the mouth, the movement of the lips and so on. An illustration of minimal pairs to assist students in pronouncing the sounds in question is as follows:

sheep	ship
key	kid
feel	fill
leak	lick
seek	sick
seat	sit
heat	hit

Numerous minimal pair lists involving about 25 different languages can be found in *Pronunciation Contrasts in English* by Don and Alleen Nilson.[15] Much of the information presented on minimal pairs in the current writing was gathered from the Nilsons. Sounds in three languages selected for illustration which can be expected to give ESOL students difficulty, and for which minimal pair pronunciation contrasts would be recommended are as follows.

Spanish		Russian		Hebrew	
seen	sin	seen	sin	big	beg
lick	luck	head	had	did	dad
wait	wet	map	mop	lick	luck
head	had	dull	doll	wait	wet
bench	bunch	collar	caller	bake	back
shave	sang	Sam	sang	shave	shove
match	much	whip	hip	sail	soul
map	mop	wear	where	bench	bunch
luck	look	wipe	ripe	match	much
buss	boss	free	three	map	mop
rob	robe	veil	they'll	cat	kite
collar	caller	thin	sin	dull	doll
full	fool	then	zen	luck	look
bull	bowl	gone	gong	but	boat
Sam	sang	chip	ship	buss	boss
pie	buy	jeer	cheer	god	good
whip	hip			rob	robe
wear	where			gone	gown
wait	gate			full	fool
free	three			nose	noise
vote	boat			mouse	mice
thin	tin			owl	oil

---

[15] Nilsen, D. L. F. and Nilsen, A. P. (1971). *Pronunciation contrasts in English*. New York: Simon and Schuster.

thigh	shy			me	we
thin	sin			whip	hip
then	zen			wear	where
gone	gong			wine	vine
sell	shell			free	three
sip	zip			veil	they'll
jeep	sheep			thin	tin
jeer	cheer			thigh	shy
jello	yellow			thin	tin
				then	zen
				gone	gong
				jeep	sheep
				gyp	zip
				jeer	cheer
				jello	yellow
				wig	wing

Besides the phonemes focused upon in three languages used for illustrative purposes above, what follows is a list of priority phonemes. Regardless of the mother tongue of the student, a teacher can assess individuals for phonetic difficulties by having them repeat words in each of the categories listed. Minimal pair exercises can then be prepared in a tailor made fashion for an individual or group of learners whose difficulties have been noted.

List of Priority Phonemes

With Frequent Function Words and Inflections

[m]	[ae]	[ɪ]	[y]	[ey]	[ʃ]
I' m a m M issus M ister M iss	a m a n a t th at	i t i s i n th i s M i ssus M i ster M i ss s i x	y ou y our y es Y iddish	ei ght th ey tod ay th ey 're	sh e

[uw]	[iy]	[a]	[d]	[t]	[ð]
t o t o day t o o d o y o u wh o tw o	h e sh e w e thre e w e re h e re	n o t wh a t o n a re	d o d on't d oes to d ay (VERB + ed PAST as in hugged)	t o t oo t en t oday tha t a t i t wha t no t eigh t (VERB + ed PAST as in Jumped)	th e th ese th is th at th ose th ey th ere th ey're

[s]	[ə]	[z]	[ŋ]	[r]	[n]
Mi ss us Mi s ter Mi ss That' s it' s ye s thi s s ix	a th e Mist e r Miss u s d oe sn't d oe s o ne w a s w e re	i s the s e tho s e he' s she' s ha s hi s doe s noun+ s (plural) Verb+ s (3rd pers. sing. pres.)	(VERB + ing) sing ing play ing	a r e h r e the r e you' r e they' r e whe r e we r e fo r he r Miste r th r ee	n ow n ine n o n ot i n o n seve n whe n te n

LIST of PRIORITY PHONEMES (with frequent function words and inflections)

68

CHAPTER 6

The Demise of the Audiolingual Method as the Foundation of a Course

Even in its early stages, as the Audiolingual method began to be accepted on a wider basis and gain in popularity, it seemed that cognitive learning theory proponents were apprehensive about it and viewed it as something that was out of focus. Their problem, however, was that it was difficult to quarrel with success, and the Audiolingual method was indeed showing itself to be successful. Gradually, though, criticism began to mount. It was suggested, for example, that students became bored with the mindless mechanical pattern drills presented. The repetition required by the method was also said to turn students into parrots. Although students could verbalize the patterns they were taught, they seemed unable to fashion anything creative or new. Furthermore, the method was attacked for being too teacher dominant. Student input into the learning process was neither encouraged nor accepted.

At first such criticisms were ignored, but as they gained momentum, they began to receive responses. For example, ALM advocates denied that students became bored with repetitious drills and recitations. Perhaps, they acknowledged, a teacher might become bored with repeated chantings, but ESOL students needed and very much desired to hear the material again and again. When first learning a new language's expressions, ALM defenders contended, one appreciates hearing and saying them over and over until they are internalized. Despite such robust defense arguments, there seemed no let-up from ALM critics, and some respected linguists expressed negative opinions about the matter. This gradually undermined the confidence of many Audiolingual users in the program. As new research findings were publicized and internalized, experimentation with other methods began.

There were several key factors that dislodged the Audiolingual method from mainstream usage. In the 1960s a significant change in linguistic theory began to occur as the emergence of such concepts as humanistic pedagogy in language teaching entered the scene. The humanism approach, as it was called, was based upon democratic principles such as respecting the integrity of students, allowing for their personal growth, responsibility and input into the learning process. The approach represented what was termed 'whole person learning and discovery,' as contrasted with the 'rigidity, mindless mimicry and teacher domination' of the Audiolingual method. Such ideas challenged the very foundations upon which Audiolingualism rested.

Even more significant, ALM was reproached as being unsound in terms of language and learning theory. It was especially faulted for being unable to meet the reasonable expectation of students to transfer their ALM communicative language learning to real life situations outside the classroom. Noam Chomsky's skepticism of ALM claims led to his outright rejection of the behaviorist theory and the structural teaching approach used in ALM. His theory of transformational grammar (TG) challenged the underpinnings of ALM's theory of language acquisition. The behaviorist theory, he maintained, was an inaccurate model of how people learn language because imitated and habit forming behavior is but a small part of human language. People create new forms of language by using their minds to gain insight into the knowledge underlying the abstract rules of language which they then apply. Learning language was not as behaviorism contended, the same as the kinds of learning induced through the stimulus-response—reinforcement-association mechanism. The behaviorist model, according to

Chomsky, was unsatisfactory for human language acquisition because it was not, as language learning must be, generated by the inner mental competence of the learner.

The most damaging point made about the Audiolingual method was that, in essence, its success was illusory. Since many of its learners were found unable to apply their classroom situational-theme learning to multiple situations outside it, the method achieved nothing more than producing students with language-like behaviors. The method, in other words, did nothing to promote genuine communication. ALM was then a failure in terms of generating true language acquisition. Chomsky's review of B. F. Skinner's *Verbal Behavior* in 1959 tended to sever the Audiolingual method from its tie to behavioral psychology and in turn from its scientific grounding.[16] This left the program as simply one of many, with no special claims to credibility. In 1964 Wilga Rivers analyzed the Audiolingual method in *The Psychologist and the Foreign Language Teacher* and joined Chomsky in criticizing it.[17] She concluded that instruction of grammar in one's native language is more productive in language learning than ALM instruction.

Researcher Philip Smith conducted a longitudinal study between 1965 and 1969 which made a comparison of language teaching methods. It came to be known as the Pennsylvania project because all the institutions involved in the research were located in Pennsylvania. The study's findings pointed to certain deficiencies in ALM methodology. It concluded that a traditional cognitive translation approach worked as well, if not better, than ALM, especially in certain areas. Gaining greater proficiency in reading and writing was cited as an example. Of course ALM tended to stress listening and speaking skills more so than reading and writing. The study indicated that there was no particular advantage to ALM instruction because an overall cognitive translation approach involving a student's

---

[16] Chomsky, N. (1959). Verbal Behavior by B.F. Skinner. *Language*, 26-58. Reprinted as item A-34 in the Bobbs—Merrill Reprint Series in the "Social Sciences"; in Fodor, J. A. and Katz, J. J. (1964) and in Jacobovitz, L. A. & Miron, M. S. (1967).

[17] Rivers, W.M. (1964). *The Psychologist and the Foreign Language Teacher.* TX: Univ. of Chicago Press.

first language was just as effective. Although the findings of the study were somewhat questionable, it is often cited as having entirely discredited Audiolingualism. At any rate, in the final analysis, the most popular method in the history of foreign language teaching, the Audiolingual method, was put to rest as a foundation course of language instruction.

CHAPTER 7

Post ALM Instruction

When speaking of the demise of Audiolingualism, it is important to note that this refers only to its employment in its original form as a foundation method. Portions of it, such as the repetition, substitution and backward build-up exercises are still used in many programs to facilitate language habit formation. Some ALM techniques then are still employed today in individual lessons. There are, however, linguists such as Jeremy Harmer who maintain that ALM use, even in part, is counterproductive to learners absorbing a new language. Harmer writes, "Audiolingual methodology seems to banish all forms of language processing that help students sort out new language information in their own minds."[18] The general consensus, however, appears to be that there is a need at points in a language program for habit formation instruction. Such instruction, though, should not be the end result of the program, as in ALM. It is necessary to link such habit formations to the cognitive aspects of instruction for students to benefit fully from the program and attain the desired end results.

Although elements of the Audiolingual method continued to be drawn upon, once it was considered an inadequate primary method of instruction, the question arose what to use in its stead. The Communicative language approach and humanistic

---

[18] Harmer, Jeremy. (2001). *The Practice of English*, 3rd edition pp.79-80. Essex: Pearson Education Ltd.

pedagogy were certainly in play, but neither these nor any other single method were preponderantly accepted as the most effective way to learn a new language. The same may be said of certain hybrid programs which were developed. In these, ALM-like repetition exercises were featured but augmented with lengthy and meticulous explanations of grammar. By the 1980s, a composite teaching approach was advocated in which elements of traditional and more current methods of instruction, including ALM, were combined. No particular philosophy or teaching method was endorsed as the sole answer to how best to present a new language to students. However, some merit was seen in both traditionalism and in Audiolingualism. As a result, the eclectic approach, a form of teaching that gleans from all sources, came into being. The ongoing debate and continued search for improved pedagogical language teaching methodology should be viewed as the concern and domain of those in the profession.

CHAPTER 8

ESOL Testing

During the past two and a half decades a vast number of ESOL testing instruments came into being. Today, therefore, many fine testing tools exist to assess initial placement and measure the progress made by ESOL students. However, at the time the popular and widely used Audiolingual method was in vogue, fewer testing measures were available. In the current section of this writing, rather than list and compare the numerous ESOL tests now available, the focus will be on the time period in which programs created their own tests and began to seek wider testing options. Those interested in exploring the current testing materials, some of which incorporate computer technology, can easily accomplish this by an Internet search for *ESL testing*. The worldwide organization TESOL (Teachers of English to Students of Other Languages) has also published a book entitled *ESL Tests and Testing*.[19] It describes twenty currently used language tests and discusses methods to evaluate such instruments.

In the earlier period referred to when fewer ESOL testing materials existed, necessity required that some form of evaluation be implemented. In New York City the federally funded Board of Education Adult Education Program at first had the responsibility of establishing and supervising ESOL classes

---

[19] Stoynoff, S. and Chappelle, C. (2005). *ESL Tests and Testing.* Alexandria, VA.: TESOL pub.

in the public schools and in community based organizations (CBOs). Under Title III of President John F. Kennedy's Anti-Poverty legislation, funding was accorded to each state for distribution to local educational agencies (LEAs) to establish literacy and ESOL classes for adults. The New York City Board of Education was the recognized LEA there. Funding for New York ESOL programs, therefore, went from the federal government in Washington DC to the New York State education department in Albany, New York, then to the New York City Board of Education. With these funds the board provided services such as ESOL classes, administrators, teachers, counselors, books and supplies, but no direct monetary funding to CBOs. However, The Adult Education Act, passed at a later period, allowed for direct state funding to CBOs. Hence the Board of Education attempted to determine which commercial testing materials would be suitable for program needs. At the same time, its staff development team experimented with original tests of its own. One such test was the native language reading screening test.

A. The Native Language Reading Screening Test

Whether a student was literate or illiterate in his native language was helpful to know for instructional purposes. To this end a procedure was established for rapidly determining a student's ability to read in his native tongue. New York City as a microcosm of the world has students enrolled in its ESOL classes from almost every language group. Such diversity, however, did not pose a serious problem in determining native reading ability. To serve this diverse population, newspapers in most foreign languages can be purchased from numerous city newsstands. Simply requesting a student to read aloud from a newspaper in the language he speaks was enough to determine his ability to read in his native language. The tester may not have understood what the student was reading but could easily determine whether he was reading fluently or stumbling or struggling in an attempt to sound out each word phonetically.

B. University of Michigan Tests

In the New York City adult education programs the *Lado English Series* textbooks were elected for use.[20] The University of Michigan's English Language Institute with which Robert Lado had been associated was contacted to learn more about the ESOL instruments developed there. Two of its tests proved of particular interest.

The Michigan Test of Aural Comprehension was designed to test students' ability to understand spoken English.[21] Students were given an answer booklet which contained three choices for each question asked. They were told to listen first to the question asked by the tester and to further listen as the tester read all three answer choices aloud before they marked their selection.

For example, the instructor would ask: Are you a student?

And students would choose and mark their answer sheets from given choices such as:

a. Yes, I am.
b. Yes, you are.
c. Yes, he is

An advantage of this tool was that many students could be tested at the same time. This however did not work well because of the tendency for students to look to the tester himself or to one another for a clue as to which answer to select.

---

[20] Lado, R. (1970). *Lado English Series*. NYC: Regents Publishing Co., Inc.
[21] Upshur, J., Spaan, M. and Thrasher, R. (1969). *Michigan Test of Aural Comprehension*. Michigan: The English Language Institute of the University of Michigan.

A second test, the **English Placement Test**[22] was developed a few years later. Four areas of English were tested with this instrument. They were listening comprehension, vocabulary, grammar and reading comprehension. This test was more comprehensive than the previous one. More areas such as reading comprehension were evaluated. This instrument too had the advantage of being able to test many students simultaneously. At the same time however, both instruments were too lengthy to administer on an individual basis. In addition the second test as the first, failed to address the problem of students looking to others for answers. The English Placement test was piloted by a group of ESOL instructors in the Adult education Program supervised by the author of the current writing. Feedback from the instructors was that the test might be useful for evaluating differences among advanced ESOL students but that a different instrument should be sought to evaluate beginners.

C. Informal Individual ESOL Placement Questions

The need existed in adult education programs for an initial placement test which could rapidly measure the listening and speaking levels of new ESOL enrollees. Until an adequate test could be found or developed a temporary solution was needed. At that time the author of the current writing trained teachers in the program he supervised to ascertain a student's aural-oral ESOL level in not more than five minutes. This was accomplished by informally asking students several pre-determined questions.

The first set of questions was to determine the student's ability to understand (but not necessarily to produce) basic spoken English. All of the five questions asked (such as "Are you married?") could be answered with a simple yes or no. If the instructor judged the responses to be inadequate, the

---

[22] English Placement Test by Mary Spaana and Laura Strowe; Testing and Certification Division of the English Language Institute University of Michigan, 1

student was considered as being on ESOL Level 1 and further questioning was unnecessary. If on the other hand the student responded correctly on four of the five questions, a second set of questions was asked. These were for the purpose of finding out if the student could speak simple grammatically correct English besides understanding it. Questions such as "Where were you born?" and "With whom do you live?" might be asked. One who responded adequately to most of the questions was considered to be a Level 2 ESOL speaker. Those in this category were therefore asked an additional open-ended question. They were encouraged to answer it in several sentences. One who responded by producing several grammatically correct English sentences smoothly was as a result considered an advanced or Level 4 ESOL speaker. Those who responded in broken or continuous grammatically incorrect English or who spoke haltingly were considered to be intermediate or Level 3 ESOL speakers. An example of an open-ended question asked might be one such as "Why are you interested in learning English?" or "Tell me about your family". By analyzing student responses to the kinds of questions described above, teachers were more aware of what level of ESOL instruction was needed for each student.

D. The John Test

The John Test was designed as an oral test for the purpose of determining placement of non-English speaking students.[23] It was originally developed at regional opportunity centers under the City University of New York by ESOL teachers. The test is administered on an individual basis using a series of pictures. The test is composed of three parts, with each part assessing different language skill. The first part tests oral communication, the second the ability to produce connected discourse in the form of a past tense narrative and the third (an optional part if time permits) the ability to ask questions.

---

[23] The John Test. (n.d.). Ray Kesper et al. New York, N.Y. Language Innovations, Inc.

The first two parts were deemed sufficient to discover proper placement of students at four ascending levels. It was said that the full test takes about ten minutes to administer, but a shorter version of it requires less time. The test itself consisted of seven illustrations depicting several ordinary happenings experienced by a man designated as "John". The first illustration depicts John getting out of bed.

The second shows John on a bus. Illustration three of the test shows John in a classroom. In illustration four John is seen speaking with an instructor. In illustration five John is seated at a restaurant counter ordering food. In the sixth illustration John is seen speaking to a clerk in a haberdashery store. In the final illustration John is seen sleeping in his bed in the evening. Students taking the John Test are asked present, past and future questions about the illustrations. The tester marks a score sheet for each answer generated.

In New York State, where the need for cross-program evaluation and comparison prevailed, the John Test gained the favor of state education authorities. They in turn mandated its use for student placement and evaluative purposes in all state federally funded ESOL programs. Although initially thought of as a temporary measure until an even better instrument was found or produced, in actuality the John Test became entrenched in the evaluative process. This made sense if one considers that after data was collected and recorded statewide over a period of time, based on the John Test, a reluctance to revert to a new instrument was not surprising. To replace the John Test with another and begin collecting data in a different way was considered undesirable and unnecessary. As a result the John Test remained the standard method of ESOL oral evaluation with little likelihood of change.

E. The GOSIKA English Language Oral Proficiency Examination

In the 1970s, large numbers of Jewish immigrants made their way from the USSR to Israel as well as to the United

States. Of those who chose to immigrate to America, many settled in New York City where they sought the aid of community based organizations and social service agencies that were prepared to assist them. At that time the author of the present writing worked for such an institution. Counseling, job placement and training as well as ESOL classes were made available to the newcomers. Learning English was particularly important and a necessity for most interested in finding employment. Many of those seeking professional employment had some familiarity with the English language, but it was obvious that there were gaps in their knowledge. If these gaps could be precisely identified, instructional time could then be used to focus exclusively upon them. Movement from the classroom to a job might then be accelerated in a significantly smaller time frame. Since no known instrument existed at the time to generate the needed information in a way the program preferred, a decision was made to investigate the possibility of compiling a test that would do so. After consulting with university personnel with expertise in statistics and in the field of testing, work began on the creation of the GOSIKA English Language Oral Proficiency Examination.

The GOSIKA exam was designed to Individually test students on their aural-oral knowledge of English. It was constructed in a way that the communication process was broken down into eight basic skills, each of which was tested on its own. If the criterion of movement from one level to the next one was satisfied, four ascending levels of English were attainable on the test where the following skills were evaluated:

1. Oral reception
2. Repeating verbatim
3. Oral production
4. Article usage
5. Question formation
6. Negation
7. Comparison
8. Free expression

Two statistically equivalent test forms were developed for exam use so that students retested at a later time would not be tested on the same form twice. Plans were made to develop more such forms, but for multiple reasons these did not materialize.

The rationale for the test, an explanation of its skills, its normed levels, statistical explanations, instructions for its administration and scoring system are included in the testing information which follows. In addition, Form A of the exam and the illustrations needed to answer some of its questions are included.

GOSIKA
INTRODUCTION AND RATIONALE

The purpose of this test is to evaluate the student's knowledge of basic structures of English. It does not attempt to determine vocabulary level or the student's ability to learn vocabulary effectively because they are not the most crucial tasks for the language learner. To succeed in learning a language, the student must acquire the structures of the language. Structures are learned more slowly than vocabulary because the latter is similar to "list learning," while structures acquisition is more complex. The structures which have truly been internalized by the learner are not likely to be forgotten because what has been learned is not a finite set of sentences or items but an underlying principle for the production of an infinite set of sentences. For this reason, the test concentrates on determining the structural knowledge of the student using vocabulary taken from the lowest levels of the most frequently used words of the language.

This test is an individual oral test which focuses exclusively on aural-oral ability. The reading and writing skills are based upon and are secondary to the aural-oral skills in the learning process. Very often a written measure of linguistic ability is used to evaluate the total language ability of the learner. A written measure is frequently misleading because it tells little about the speaker's listening or speaking ability. Listening and speaking are primary skills both in terms of language learning and simple survival. Although written measures of linguistic ability may be useful and important, there is no correlation necessarily between a written test and the primary oral skills, and therefore, an oral test is far preferable to a written one for initial and follow-up evaluation of an ESL student.

GOSIKA is unique among oral tests of ESL in that it breaks down the communication process into specific basic aural-oral skills. This enables one to use the test both for ESL class placement and diagnosis of specific problems. Other unique features of the test include an objective and simple scoring system and testing procedures that require no reading or writing at all (not even the filling out of an answer sheet) on the part of the test taker. Furthermore, the test scoring system takes into account the frustration level of the student by making administration of more advanced sections of the test contingent upon *successful* completion of less advanced segments of the test. This prevents a student from being forced to complete portions of the examination which are beyond his ability. Most commercially prepared ESL tests require considerable expenditures of money for the purchase of component parts such as individual student test booklets and separate booklets for the different test forms. GOSIKA differs from these in that it can be used relatively inexpensively through the optional purchase of detached individual scoring sheets. An explanation for the inclusion of the test items follows.

I. RECEPTION

In order to proceed with any testing or teaching procedure, one must first determine whether the student understands simple spoken English. By testing for physical, rather than verbal responses, we are able to determine understanding without the confusion that is sometimes associated with grammatical or incomprehensible responses. It is not always clear form verbal responses whether or not the student has understood the cue. Physical responses, however, are unambiguous and leave a clear impression of the level of knowledge.

II. REPEATING VERBATIM

If learners are able to repeat what they have heard, it is indicative that they have perceived it correctly. The ability to listen effectively is both a necessary skill in the acquisition of a new language and a good measure of the aural-oral level of the listener. This section tests primarily for the learner's ability to perceive and repeat the present tense, past tense, and present progressive tense endings without the aid of redundancy clues such as **every day** and **now**.

III. PRODUCTION

This section tests for simple production skills, namely, the ability to produce simple declarative sentences of English. It cannot be assumed that because students understand simple English, they are able to produce it at the same level. Comprehension almost invariably is at a higher level than production.

This section is divided into two parts: simple, identification of objects and the production of simple, common structures in response to verbal cues.

IV. ARTICLE USAGE

Knowledge of correct article usage is often difficult for the second language learner (although the level of difficulty for this skill varies from speech community to speech community). Incorrect article usage is an important factor in marking the learner's speech as foreign.

This section tests for the student's ability to perceive whether or not articles are being used correctly. By testing for perception rather than usage, the possibility of performance errors is eliminated, and it is possible to determine whether or not the student has a systematic approach to separating correct sentences from incorrect ones.

V. QUESTION FORMATION

Question formation is a necessary skill for eliciting information in any language. It is a complex process, involving subject-auxiliary inversion, knowledge of **wh-** words and the ability to insert these words, the modal **do** (or other modals) appropriately. This section tests for the ability to form simple questions involving the use of the copula **be** and the modal **do** in their various forms, as well as more complex questions involving the use of **wh-** words.

VI. NEGATION

Negation is a basic necessity for communication in any language. In the English language, negation involves knowing how to use the modal **do** in the simple present and past tenses and how to insert **not** correctly in the progressive tenses. The ability to do this indicates a relatively sophisticated level of English language ability.

VII. COMPARISON

This section tests the student's ability to comprehend and produce structures involving the comparatives and superlatives of regular adverbs. Knowledge of the comparative construction enriches the student's ability to specify and describe objects. This ability considerably increases the speaker's descriptive range.

In order to produce comparisons of the above form, the student must be able to decline regular adjectives correctly and insert either the definite article **the** (in the superlative form) or the word **than** (in the comparative form).

VIII. FREE EXPRESSION

This section rates the overall speaking ability of the student. The tester is asked to look for the level of fluency with which speakers express themselves in English. (Fluency is defined here in terms of speed, ease and general clarity of expression). Frequently, although the learner's speech may contain a large number of errors, they are able to communicate effectively in English.

As the judgment made in this section is a subjective one, its point value (and effect on the total score) is low.

NORMS

The GOSIKA test is in the process of being more fully normed on a large, adult Russian immigrant population.[24] Only tentative oral class placement levels can, therefore, be recommended. The publishers and authors welcome reports on matters such as the norms that users of this instrument may set in other programs and the student populations involved, comparative scores, and correlations with other ESL instruments, and so forth. The tentative norms established to date are as follows:

---

[24] Although this was originally so, it was discontinued when the test was withdrawn from use.

PERCENT SCORE:	
85 to 100	**ADVANCED ENGLISH SPEAKER** At this level, an individual can function in a work situation comparable to that of a native speaker although instruction in areas such as idiomatic expression and practice in free expression may still be needed.
70 to 84	**INTERMEDIATE ENGLISH SPEAKER** At this level, an individual can understand most of what is spoken. With hard work, persons at this level may be able to succeed if placed in a situation where they must function with native English speakers. In addition to the difficulties that an advanced speaker may encounter, an intermediate speaker can also be expected to make some errors when engaging in simple conversation and improperly employ grammatical forms that were learned (but not internalized as part of the grammar) when generating speech. A person at this level may also speak in a hesitant manner.

55 to 69	**TRANSITIONAL ENGLISH SPEAKER** An individual's ability to understand and speak is very limited at this level. Considerable work in ESL is needed before a student in this category can be expected to function adequately in a verbal situation with native English speakers. The following problems are not uncommon: not fully understanding instructions, requests or information questions, not being able to generate more than very simple, grammatically correct English sentences, making numerous tense errors, speaking in fragments where complete sentences are more appropriate, speaking haltingly or pausing frequently for long periods in an attempt to find words.
0 to 54	**NON-ENGLISH SPEAKER** An individual at this level is unable to understand most simple spoken English. Very basic ESL instruction is needed for people in this category. Areas requiring instruction are basic listening skills such as distinguishing between phonemes and repeating simple sentences, forming simple sentences, responding to simple informational questions and so forth.

VALIDITY

The test purports to measure the student's receptive and productive abilities in the English language. The test items were constructed so as to require the student to perform specific tasks. The validity of such a construction is obvious — the tester simply observes the student to monitor the performance of the required tasks. Without a clear understanding of what is said, the tasks cannot be performed correctly.

Another criterion of validity used was the rating of judges. Two groups, one consisting of seven professional staff members (4 teachers and 3 counselors), and the second of 30 fellow ESL students were employed. Members of both these groups had been in daily contact with the test takers for at least 8 weeks. The judges were asked to give their opinion of the test takers' listening and speaking abilities in English. A combined rating for each group of judges was obtained. A correlation of .84 was found between the test and the professional group's rating, and one of .85 between the test and the student group's rating. The correlations between the test and judges ratings are sufficient to consider the test valid.

RELIABILITY

Reliability answers the question: How self-consistent is the test? Will students, for example, who obtain high scores on one occasion, in general obtain high scores on a second taking? If the rank order of test scores differs markedly in a second administration than the order obtained in the first, the test may not be considered useful as an index of a particular test taker's ability. The reliability of this test was obtained by correlating Form A with Form B. ESL instruction did not occur between the administration of both forms. The reliability coefficient obtained was .90 with a standard error of .03. This score indicates that the test clearly meets the requirements of self-consistency and is, therefore, a reliable instrument.

GENERAL INSTRUCTIONS

Each section of the test (with the exception of Sections VI and VIII) contains example sentences, sample sentences and test items. Example sentences are used by the tester to demonstrate the required task and may be repeated as often as necessary. Sample sentences are used to determine whether the students have correctly understood the instructions. If they perform a sample task correctly, the tester may proceed with the test items. If not, the tester should repeat the instructions and demonstrate the example sentence once more. The tester should then have the student try the sample task again.

For example, in Section II, Repeating Verbatim, the sample sentence is, "I have a nice apartment." The tester says to the student: "If I say, 'I have a nice apartment,' you must say, 'I have a nice apartment.' Let's try it with another sentence." At this point, the sample sentence is used. The tester says the sample sentence and then gestures to the student to perform the task (in this case, repeating the sentence word for word).

Sections I, III and VII require the use of props and pictures as cues. Props should be neatly assembled on the desk or table in front of the tester. For Section I (Reception) – Form A, the tester needs the following props: a nickel, a piece of paper, a book, a pencil and a key. For Form B, the tester needs the following props: a dime, a pen, a book, a pencil and a key. For Section III (Production) – Form A, the tester needs pictures #2, 4, 5 and the following props: a pen and a piece of paper. For Form B, the tester needs pictures #1, 2, 3, 6 and the following prop: a pencil. For Section VII, the tester needs pictures #6, 7 and 8.

NOTE: Before administering the test, the tester should have the picture cues at hand for use in Sections III and VII. The scoring sheet should also be at hand for scoring as the test proceeds.

The test is administered according to the section outline given below:

I   Reception
II Repeating Verbatim
III Production
IV Article Usage

V   Question Formation
VI   Negation
VII Comparison
VIII Free Expression

Students may not proceed to Section II of the test unless they have attained a raw score of at least 5 on Section I. they may not proceed to Section III unless they have attained a raw score of at least 12 on Section II. Having passed Section II, the student may proceed in the test through all the remaining sections with the exception of VIII. In order to proceed to Section VIII, the student must have achieved an overall raw score of 60.

In administering the test, the tester should:

a) Make sure to speak clearly and naturally (neither too rapidly nor too slowly).

b) Not allow the student to see the written test items.

c) Read both the general and specific instructions as well as the instructions for scoring before administering the test.

d) A tester that finds it necessary to repeat the instructions for the student should try to explain the instructions using different simpler ways of expressing that which the student fails to understand.

e) In scoring the test, the tester should be aware that self-correction (if students correct themselves without help) is to be counted as a completely correct answer and should be scored accordingly.

f) The tester must listen carefully to student responses. If unsure that the student has performed the task exactly as required, the student should be asked to repeat the response.

g) In monitoring student responses, the tester should be aware that a response of "I don't know" at any point in the test, unless immediately self-corrected, receives a score of 0.

h) The tester must not indicate by gesture, verbal or facial expression that the student is performing the task successfully or unsuccessfully. Testers must beware of the student's natural tendency to look for assurance and of their own natural tendency to give it.

Test Booklet Form A

It is strongly recommended that the tester thoroughly read the GOSIKA test manual, especially the section entitled General Instructions, before proceeding to use this test booklet.

I RECEPTION

PROPS: A nickel, a piece of paper, a book, a pencil, a key.
The props should be assembled neatly in front of the tester. Use the props as indicated for eliciting student responses.

NOTE: After students perform a task such as #7 or #8, inform them that they may sit down again or put down whatever item they are holding.

SCORING: Each item – 1 point.
Score students on appropriateness of response. If the student is asked to pick up a pen, and does so, the response is scored as correct. If they do nothing or pick up something else, or put the pen down instead of picking it up, the response receives no credit.

RECEPTION
Example: Pick up the pencil.
Sample: Pick up the key.

(A)
   1) Pick up the nickel.
   2) Put it on the paper.
   3) Give me the book.
   4) Place the nickel under the paper.
   5) Raise your right hand.
   6) Show me the door.
   7) Please stand up.
   8) Please open the book.

II REPEATING VERBATIM

The tester should ask the student to repeat the sentences *exactly* as heard. Give each cue once, clearly. Do not repeat any test item.

SCORING: Each item – 2 points
Score the student's response as correct only in the event that the student repeats the test item exactly as stated.

NOTE: Contractions are acceptable, and responses containing contractions should receive full credit. For example, if a student says, "I'm a doctor" instead of "I am a doctor," the response is acceptable.

REPEATING VERBATIM

Example: **I have a nice apartment.** ("I have a nice apartment.")
Sample: **He is a good doctor.** ("He is a good doctor" or "He's a good doctor.")

(A)
1) I eat breakfast at 7:30.
2) She works in Manhattan.
3) You helped me wash the dishes.
4) You are reading a newspaper.
5) They lived in Israel for five years.
6) He drives a car.
7) We like coffee with milk and sugar.
8) She is eating meat for supper.

III PRODUCTION:

PROPS: A pen, a piece of paper
Testers should have these props and the pictures assembled neatly in front of them. Use the prop and picture cues as

indicated for eliciting student response. Give each cue once initially. Cues may be repeated only one more time.

SCORING: Each item – 1 point
Score students on appropriateness *and* grammaticality of response. If students are asked to identify an object and do so accurately and grammatically (even in a two-word utterance such as "a pen"), the response is given full credit. If they identify the object as something it is not, or identify it accurately but ungrammatically (for example, by saying "pen" or "Is a pen" or "This a pen") the response receives no credit.

PRODUCTION
Example: What is this? (a pencil) "This is a pencil."
Sample: What is this? (a book) "This is a book." "It's a book," or "A book."

What is this? (telephone)
What are these? (clocks)
What is he? (doctor, man)
What is today's date?
What time is it in the picture? (11:15)
What's your address?
Where is the pen? (on the paper)

IV ARTICLE USAGE

The tester should ask the student to label the following sentences as correct or incorrect sentence of English (or good or bad sentence of English). Give each cue once. Repeat the cue once more if necessary.

NOTE: In this section, students tend to think out loud about the sentences. If necessary, remind the student that they need only answer correct or good or incorrect or bad.

SCORING: Each item – 1 point

Score students on whether or not they correctly identify incorrect sentences as bad and correct sentences as good. The student is not to be scored on whether or not this information is communicated grammatically.

ARTICLE USAGE
Sample: I bought shoes. (**correct** or **good**)
I bought a shoes. (**incorrect** or **bad**)
Example: I go home on weekends. (**correct** or **good**)
I go home a weekends. (**incorrect** or **bad**)

1) I ate the sandwiches.
2) I heard a good news.
3) I like a cars.
4) We met a Johnsons.
5) I saw the stores.
6) The teachers are in school.
7) I know a men.
8) The children came home.
9) A clothes are clean.
10) Some people are good.

V QUESTION FORMATION

The tester should tell students to ask the questions listed below. Give each cue once initially. Repeat once more if necessary.

SCORING: Each item – 1 point
Student responses are to be evaluated on the basic of grammaticality. Only completely
grammatically correct responses are to be given credit.

QUESTION FORMATION
Example: Ask me what my name is. ("What is your name?" or "What's your name?")
Sample: Ask me if I speak English. ("Do you speak English?")

1) Ask me what time it is. (What time is it?")
2) Ask me if I like America. ("Do you like America?")
3) Ask me if I am a teacher. ("Are you a teacher?")
4) Ask me if the doctor lives in New York. ("Does the doctor live in New York?")
5) Ask me if the room is big. ("Is the room big?")
6) Ask me where I live. (Where do you live?")
7) Ask me when the bus comes. ("When does the bus come?")
8) Ask me when I came to work. ("When did you come to work?")
9) Ask me where the teacher went. ("Where did the teacher go?")
10) Ask me where the student was born. ("Where was the student born?")
11) Ask me if I ate lunch. ("Did you eat lunch?")

VI NEGATION:

The tester should ask the student to change these sentences from positive to negative (or "yes" or "no"). give each cue twice initially. Repeat once more if necessary.

SCORING: Each item – 1 point
Student responses are to be evaluated on the basic of grammaticality and the precision of sentence repetition. If the student performs the negation correctly but makes a mistake in repeating another part of the sentence, no credit is given for the response. (For example, if the student says: "She is not a good doctor." instead of "He is..." no credit is given for the response.)

NOTE: As in Section 2 (**Repeating Verbatim**) contractions are acceptable.

NEGATION:
1) Example: I like coffee. ("I don't like coffee," or "I do not like coffee.")

2) Sample: We are engineers. ("We are not engineers," or "We aren't engineers.)"
3) He is a good doctor. ("He is not a good doctor.")
4) They go to school. ("They do not go to school.")
5) She eats lunch at 12:00. ("She does not eat lunch at 12:00.")
6) He paid for it. ("He did not pay for it.")
7) We are listening to the radio. ("We are not listening to the radio.")
8) She is a good teacher. ("She is not a good teacher.")
9) They drive to work. ("They do not drive to work.")
10) He works in Brooklyn. ("He does not work in Brooklyn.")
11) They rented an apartment. ("They did not rent an apartment.")
12) She is writing a letter. ("She is not writing a letter.")

VII COMPARISON

The tester should have the pictures at hand. Point to the pictures indicated by number for eliciting student responses.

SCORING:
Each comprehension item – 1 point
Each production item – 3 point
For comprehension items, any accurate response to the cue, whether verbal or non-verbal, grammatical or ungrammatical, is given full credit. If the student correctly identifies the bigger car or the tallest man (in any way), full credit is given.
For production items, the students response must be completely grammatical, as well as accurate, in order to receive credit in scoring.

COMPARISON

Comprehension
1) Picture #6. Show me the bigger car.

2) Picture #7. Show me the shortest man.

3) Picture #7. Show me the happiest man.

Production

1) Picture #6.

Tester says: Car A is bigger than Car B.

Tell me about these cars using the word "smaller."

2) Picture #7.

Tester says: Man A is the tallest man in this picture.

Tell me about these three men using the word "shortest."

VII FREE EXPRESSION

The tester should choose 3 of the following 6 topics and encourage the student to respond at length.

SCORING:

Assign a score of 0-4 to the student's response on the basis of fluency, namely speed, ease and general clarity of expression. In this section, the tester should not place too much weight on student errors unless they render the student's speech incomprehensible or glaringly foreign.

FREE EXPRESSION

1) Tell me about your family.

2) Tell me about your trip to America.

3) Tell me about your native country.

4) Tell me what you like about the United States/New York City.

5) Tell me what you don't like about the United States/New York City.

6) Tell me about your profession.

GOSIKA PICTURES

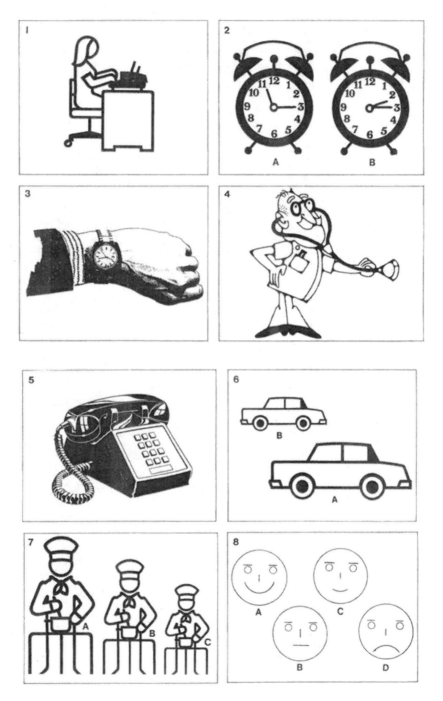

GOSIKA

INDIVIDUAL STUDENT SCORING SHEET

STUDENT'S NAME: FORM:

LAST,   FIRST   M.I.   (A or B)

DATE: TESTER:

MONTH   DAY   YEAR   NAME

I RECEPTION	II REPEATING VERBATIM	III PRODUCTION	IV ARTICLE USAGE
1	1	1	1
2	2	2	2
3	3	3	3
4	4	4	4
5	5	5	5
6	6	6	6
7	7	7	7
8	8	SUB TOTAL_____	8
SUB TOTAL_____	SUB TOTAL_____		9
DO NOT PROCEED TO THE NEXT SECTION UNLESS THE STUDENT HAS OBTAINED A RAW SCORE OF AT LEAST 5 ON THIS SECTION.	DO NOT PROCEED TO THE NEXT SECTION UNLESS THE STUDENT HAS OBTAINED A RAW SCORE OF AT LEAST 12 ON THIS SECTION.		10
			SUB TOTAL_____

V QUESTION FORMATION	VI NEGATION	VII COMPARISON	VIII FREE EXPRESSION
1	1	COMPREHENSION	(CIRCLE ONE)
2	2	1	0 1 2 3 4
3	3	2	SUB TOTAL_____
4	4	3	SUB TOTALS
5	5	SUB TOTAL _____	I
6	6	PRODUCTION	II
7	7	1	III
8	8	2	IV
9	9	SUB TOTAL _____	V
10	10	DO NOT PROCEED TO THE NEXT SECTION UNLESS THE SUBTOTAL SCORES EQUAL A RAW SCORE OF AT LEAST 60.	VI
11	SUB TOTAL _____		VII
SUB TOTAL _____			VIII

TOTAL RAW SCORE

PERCENTAGE
(SEE CONVERSION TABLE)

After the GOSIKA test was successfully piloted in the program of its origin, it was submitted to New York State program monitors for consideration for use as an alternative to the John test. After deliberation, however, a decision to continue monitoring aural-oral progress with the John test was made. What appeared to play heavily on this decision was the factor referred to previously of not wishing to change the existent data gathering system. Nevertheless, the program that had created the GOSIKA was permitted to use it in place of the John but with a stipulation. The latter involved correlating GOSIKA scores with those of the John test for reporting and data collection purposes. This was done for a period of time but ultimately discontinued. As other community based organizations (CBOs) began contacting the agency using the GOSIKA for information about how they too might replace the John test with it, the parent agency that had permission to do so grew concerned. Its dealings with the state were numerous, and the agency did not wish to be viewed as pushing or encouraging other organizations to use the GOSIKA instrument rather than the one the state preferred. It was not in their interest to be seen as competing with the state over the selection of testing materials. As a result, the agency's ESOL program reverted to the use of the John test, and the GOSIKA instrument was taken out of circulation. Plans that had been made to publicize and promote the use of the GOSIKA were, therefore, abandoned.

CHAPTER 9

Culture: a Significant Factor in Language Learning

Regardless of the method employed to teach a new language, it is necessary to take into account the cultural background of the students being taught. Culture in the narrower sense of the term has been defined as the literature, art and music typical of a given group. However, this definition excludes the group's value system, mores and customs, which are certainly also crucial components. A definition of culture that would seem more appropriate is given by M. V. Zintz. He defines culture in the broader sense as "the totality of the way of life of a group." This totality includes the religious, family, educational, governmental, recreational and economic structure of a group. Finocchiaro in addition points out that "Anthropologists' studies have emphasized that language is the central feature of culture."[25]

When a new language is learned, the culture of those who use that language is also conveyed. In pluralistic American society newcomers almost always take pride in their heritage and hopefully will absorb and integrate American culture with their own. It is not unusual for people who are part of the U.S.A. to identify themselves not merely as American, but as American preceded by a hyphen. The country, therefore, consists of

---

[25] Zintz, M. V. (1963). *Education Across Cultures*. Dubuque, Iowa: William C. Brown Book Company.

African-Americans, Greek-Americans, Italian-Americans, Hispanic-Americans, Irish-Americans, and so forth. People from all such groups relate to their original culture but at the same time share the broader American one.

Students who are connected to the culture of their ancestry and feel secure with it possess the tools to negotiate and incorporate a new culture into their lives without a sense of loss or fear of losing or giving up a background in which they take pride. On the other hand, those who are insecure because they sense an effort is being made to remove their native ways from them are more likely to resist coming to terms with and incorporating the dominant culture which now surrounds them in a positive way.

In the United States when English is taught to newcomers, instructors must be careful not to belittle or give the impression that their students' original culture must be completely abandoned and replaced by the American one. Rather, one should attempt to convey that in a democratic country such as the U.S.A., students are free to function culturally both monolithically as well as pluralistically. On one hand, they can continue to be proud of and retain their native culture, while at the same time learning and integrating the culture of their newly adopted country. Within their own ethnic group they should not feel they will be criticized or faulted by relating to one another monolithically in the culture of their birth. At the same time, knowledge of American ways will permit newcomers to understand and respond to others outside their ethnic group, pluralistically, in terms of what is shared by all Americans.

It would be a grave error to conclude that cultural attachment need not be considered or plays no more than a minor role in language learning. That cultural identification is a sensitive and potentially explosive issue can be seen by clashes between groups in different parts of the world. These often result from ethnic groups who fear the majority population among whom they live do not respect or are attempting to destroy their culture. The Kurds in Turkey, the Basques in Spain, the followers of the Dali Lama in China, the French-speaking population of Canada are but a few examples of this universal phenomenon. This is not to say that a revolution or violent explosion will erupt in a class if the students' native culture is minimized or ignored. Rather, it is that the attitude of students toward the English language and the American way of life may be negatively affected. The English language under such circumstances may be learned for practical purposes but at the same time resented internally. This could result in the refusal of students to voluntarily integrate into the larger American society.

There is no place in an English language class for rules or comments such as: "There is to be no speaking a foreign language in this classroom," or "If you have anything to say to anyone here, you are only permitted to say it in English." Such directives are hurtful and intimidating to new language students and fail to enhance learning in a constructive manner. They convey the impression that there is something wrong with the language the students are accustomed to, as well as with the culture from which they stem. It is of course necessary to encourage English speaking. However, private discourse between students themselves in their native language (which often involves reviewing or more deeply clarifying the teaching material) need not be regulated or interfered with.

In contrast to the above, English language programs can be helpful and greatly appreciated by students of other cultures. Programs can find ways to provide students with the resources and opportunities to look deeper into their roots in some instances. People may, for example, be desirous of studying their own history in greater detail and perhaps learn more about aspects of their culture which were unknown to them in the past. In other words, gaps in the students' knowledge of their own collective past may be filled in this way. Such an approach is particularly desirable for students whose full native culture may have intentionally been denied them, and who are seeking the opportunity to repair this deficiency. Students who were trapped in countries ruled by totalitarian and hostile regimes may fall into such a category.

That students will respond more positively to learning English and accept the American way of life if they are assisted to find answers they may have about their own background is based on an assumption. Namely, those knowledgeable and secure in the mores, folkways, ethos and history of their people are more likely to entertain and absorb a new culture successfully. In a way, it may be considered comparable to teaching students who are illiterate in their native languages to read in English. Although it is not always practical to do so, ideally, teaching these students to read in their native languages could be expected to accelerate the goal of reading in English. Learning to read in their native language will make more sense to them, reduce barriers and enhance their ability to master English reading.

In the narrative that follows, a group of students from the former Soviet Union who were denied the right to learn more about or practice their culture is discussed. It is pointed out that certain measures can be taken in the process of teaching English that would assist such people to satisfy their craving to learn more about their past. Such actions, it is suggested, will ultimately result in students being more comfortable in negotiating the process of Americanization. Although the events described occurred in a faith-based social service agency, it should be noted that the participants involved came solely for the purpose of learning English. The specific suggestions made for this group, though not universally applicable, should be viewed as examples of how any English language program might develop tailor-made activities to assist students to find answers to or explore their antecedence more deeply. The availability of such opportunities will demonstrate that students need not fear that the goal of English language instruction is to destroy or wean them from their native culture. Such sensitivity to the students' grounding can be expected to make them more receptive to learning English and the American culture which encompasses it.

In 1985 after studying English for several weeks at a New York City Jewish social service organization, one student, an immigrant from the former Soviet Union, mustered enough courage to ask his teacher: "Why do you call us Russians here? In Russia they called us Jews." This comment reflected the feeling that Jewish newcomers from the Soviet Union were not being accepted as such by the American Jewish community. It would have been an error to dismiss this feeling as having existed only among a small percentage of the more than 120,000 Jews who had arrived in America at that time since 1970. Indications were that the vast majority of these newcomers harbored this view and, in fact, were correct. They had not become integrated with American Jewry. Their sense of anomy—that they were living in a no man's land culturally and psychologically—can be understood in terms of psycholinguistic and acculturative processes.

The study of sounds, structures and meanings which enable those who speak the same language to understand one another is termed linguistics. Psycholinguistics is a related term which attempts to determine the processes by which one learns a first language and subsequently acquires other languages.

Despite the extensive scientific work done in these fields, no one knows for certain how language is learned. It is known, however, that by the time children are about five years of age, they are proficient in all the important elements of the oral aspects (listening and speaking) of the language to which they have been exposed. Learning a language cannot be disassociated from learning concepts, therefore the acquisition of a second language frequently entails the revisiting of a known concept but from a new perspective. The learning of any concept involves learning to think; hence learning a language is related to the thinking system we develop. Without language our thinking would almost certainly be hampered. Despite some evidence that a certain amount of thinking goes on before speech is learned, it can hardly be disputed that a great deal of thinking is dependent on the knowledge of words. At the very least, it is probable that language not only greatly assists our thinking but also aids us in organizing ideas. One great advantage of knowing an additional language, and in turn the thinking system which automatically accompanies it, is that one is able to analyze a problem from more than a single perspective. Our language and thinking become an intrinsic part of our life, our personality and our culture. Although the language we speak is usually a component of the culture to which we belong (and some, as Finocciaro indicated, maintain that language is the central component), this did not hold true of the Soviet immigrants in question.

The key factor in any process of acculturation is social interaction. It is this factor which prevented the Jewish immigrants from Russia, despite their knowledge of the Russian language, from integrating fully into the Soviet system. As Jews, their social interaction with other elements in the Soviet Union was restricted. As a result, though most of them knew neither of the Jewish languages (Hebrew or Yiddish) they were forcibly brought face to face with the fact that they were Jews. The fact that as Russian Jews they were never viewed (and never viewed themselves) as true Russians but were identified in Russia as "Jews" is not unique. Jews who lived in other anti-Semitic countries in the past were also deprived of full ethnic, civil and political rights. However, irrespective of this lack of citizenship rights, the Jews in these countries were able to continue to develop as Jews. Wherever Jews felt that persecution was hindering their development as Jewish individuals, they almost invariably sought to emigrate to a more hospitable environment. This was not so in the case of the Jews from the Soviet Union. In addition to being denied the possibility to develop and function as Jews, they were forbidden to emigrate. Neither accepted as full-fledged members of the Soviet entity, nor permitted to become familiar with their Jewish heritage they were beset by a sense of anomie.

Traditionally, immigrant groups that have come to the United States have related to the mainstream American culture in terms of their own national or ethnic identities. When the Americans and the immigrants adopted the assimilative melting pot theory, this process broke down, resulting in a cultural loss which was detrimental to both sides. Eventually, due to various developments resulting from World War II and its aftermath (America is no longer considered "the last best hope of mankind," and the consciousness raising of ethnic groups such as Blacks and Hispanics) the melting pot view was replaced by cultural pluralism—the belief that many different cultures could harmoniously exist side by side.

Of course, even an ethnic minority that is determined to maintain its own way of life must relate to the mainstream American culture. For example, immigrants from Greece do so as Greeks, Italians as Italians, and so forth. In other words, in order to relate to mainstream America without sacrificing one's own cultural identity as it absorbs certain mainstream components, each culture must have a secure base or support system grounded in its own heritage. Most Jews who arrived on the American scene earlier from countries where they were not accepted found a strong Jewish cultural base to attach themselves to in America. This facilitated their integration into the American culture. This was not so with the Jewish newcomers from Russia. They had neither a Russian nor a Jewish base to which to attach themselves. They were, therefore, confronted with a unique dilemma that drew them further towards anomie. They felt no kinship with the non-Jewish Russian community in the United States, they were not accepted by the English speaking community at large, and they were unable to relate as Jews to the American Jewish community.

Since the Soviet Jewish immigrants were nevertheless Jews and viewed themselves as such, but had not had the freedom to develop their culture in Russia, it was suggested that their dilemma might be solved by assisting them to develop their Jewish heritage in the free American society. Such an approach would not only enable them to experience freedom in the United States and to contrast it with the totalitarianism from which they escaped. It would also help them to form ties with the American Jewish community. Therefore, a closer linkage to American Jewry, coupled with a stronger knowledge of their Jewish heritage, would serve as the missing link from which they would be able, as other Jewish immigrant groups had done before them, to negotiate the mainstream American culture.

This is where formal and informal English as an additional language can perform an invaluable service. It can be used to integrate the Soviet Jewish immigrants into the American culture, not only without minimizing their Jewish heritage, but by broadening their cultural and psychological horizon to include the basic concepts of Judaism. Almost without exception, these Jewish immigrants desired desperately to learn English. Although the ways of the mainstream American culture are inherently conveyed through the learning of the English language, such English instruction can be structured to introduce students to elements of Jewish culture. When Jewish organizations undertake Americanization of Jewish immigrants from Russia, they might consider not relying entirely on commercial texts aimed at the wide, general American market. They might rather turn to materials that within the confines of Americanization teach the customs and practices common to Jews the world over. Although such teaching materials are not widely available, creative teachers have been known to develop their own. In addition, a start can be made in the desired direction through informal educational devices such as:

- Field trips to historical Jewish sites or unique Jewish communities such as Boro Park or Williamsburg in New York City, especially at times such as on intermediate days of Passover and Succoth (Tabernacles)
- Discussions of articles in the Anglo-Jewish press and articles of Jewish interest in the American press. Students might be encouraged to keep scrapbooks of such ideas
- Discussions of similarities and differences between classic Judaism and the concepts of western democracy
- Assembling a class library of Jewish books and articles of Jewish interest
- Meeting with resource persons who can serve as additional English language role models (well-known rabbinic personalities, Jewish lay leaders, scientists or other prominent individuals who are also actively practicing Jews)

Such an educational, bicultural—if you will—approach to English as a second language can help newcomers such as those from the Soviet Union attain that self-assurance which will enable them to become part of the American cultural scene without the conscious or unconscious sense of loss that they might otherwise experience.

CHAPTER 10

Related Questions and Answers

Question 1

Is it better to staff an ALM program with a bilingual rather than a monolingual teacher?

Answer

Actually, there are advantages to both. A teacher who is bilingual in the student's native language is able to translate certain words and phrases for the sake of clarity and then quickly move on with the planned lesson. A monolingual teacher might require more time to get an incidental point across. When, for example, a lesson is given on fruits and vegetables, the word *olive* might be mentioned. A monolingual teacher might have to search for a picture of an olive in order to explain what it is. Drawing an oval shape on the board would not be helpful since students might associate it with an egg. Finding a picture of an olive may prove more time consuming than desired. A bilingual teacher, on the other hand, has the ability to translate the word rapidly and move on from there. However, once translation comes into play, there is the danger of it being over-used and relied on too often. A monolingual teacher would not be confronted with this problem.

To paraphrase Robert Lado who was asked this question, he replied that in his many years of working in the field, he came across very good bilingual teachers, but also bad ones. At the same time, he came across both very good and poor monolingual teachers. His advice was not to make bilingualism or monolingualism the key criterion in teacher selection. When searching for a teacher, one that is good should be given priority. Being bilingual or not does not necessarily speak to the issue of teacher competence.

Question 2

Should an ALM teacher with a regional accent be hired to teach a class in another region?

Answer

It should be understood that there is no one English accent which is universally "correct." Each accent is correct for the area in which the people there employ it. This being said, ideally, students should learn to speak English in the way it is spoken in the region where they reside.

Minor variations in accent or expressions on the part of a teacher should not be viewed as a fatal or, for that matter, even as a genuine flaw.

Slight differences in regional pronunciations, such as a teacher from upstate New York using the long **a** [æ] sound in words, rather than the short **a [æ]** as in New York City, should certainly not affect employment. Nor for that matter should a teacher from an English speaking foreign country such as England generally be excluded from teaching in the USA because of certain differences in accent or colloquial expression. For example, referring to *gasoline* as *petrol* or to a *candy* as a *sweet* or to a *lollipop* as a *sucker* should essentially be viewed as insignificant. The regional usage for such terms Is generally learned rapidly and, when necessary, one can easily modify the usage.

On the other hand, it may at times be reasonable not to employ native speaking English teachers with particular forms of speech. A teacher from England, for example, who speaks with a heavy Cockney dialect in which there is extreme diphthongization of vowels, or the loss of the initial /h/ sound, or the use of an intrusive /r/ would be a poor choice for students outside such a person's region. A teacher with a very sing-song type speaking tone sometimes found in English speakers from the West Indies or India may also not be a wise choice for students from another region. The basic criterion in these matters should be to assess whether native born English speaking residents in the area where the English instruction is to take place can understand the teacher candidate with little or no difficulty. If so, employing the person should not be ruled out.

Question 3

Is it helpful to point out to students or to encourage students to point out to their teacher how their native language differs from English in sentence construction, for example, or to discuss other language dissimilarities?

Answer

A teacher must be careful about using class time for such purposes, or at least consider how much class time is taken to engage in such discussions. One must keep in mind the primary objective of focusing upon teaching the students English. Discussing how other languages relate to English may be an interesting topic, but can be detrimental if it serves as a diversion from the main goal. In other words, the teacher must understand that talking about English and how it relates to other languages is not the same as teaching English.

Question 4

Is it reasonable to assume that a student who is literate in his native language will learn to speak English more rapidly than an illiterate student?

Answer

No. On the contrary, the opposite is more likely. Literate students have been conditioned to turn to and depend on the written word when learning. In wrestling with such materials as English newspaper and magazine articles, literate students learning English might well improve their reading and perhaps to an extent their spelling and writing skills. Speaking, however, is another matter. In America and other Anglo Saxon countries, the English language may be characterized as consisting of both a formal and informal aspect. In America especially people speak informal English but tend to write in a far more formal mode. One simply does not speak the way a newspaper, magazine or book is generally written. A student can, therefore, not be expected to become proficient in informal English speech by reading formal English publications. There is no danger of course of illiterate students being dependent on the written word. By the necessity of being illiterate they have had little choice but to develop keen listening skills to function in everyday life. Since speaking a new language is dependent on hearing fine distinctions in sounds and patterns, they are usually better equipped than their literate graphic-dependent classmates to master the oral dimension of listening and speaking English. It is, therefore, not surprising to find illiterate students learning to speak English more rapidly than their literate counterparts.

Question 5

Is it correct to assume that a person with high intelligence will excel in English language learning?

Answer

Not necessarily. High intelligence does not guarantee success in becoming adept in a new language. Some people are fortunate enough to be born with a particular talent. It may, for example, be in the area of music or art. Even without special training, such people may be able to sing well or draw very skillfully. It also appears that there are individuals who are born with a talent to master additional languages easily. People with this talent are generally conversant in several languages other than their native one.

At the other end of the spectrum are people who have extreme difficulty in learning a new language. They might be compared to a tone-deaf person for whom listening to music does little. Such people may simply be called poor language learners. Generally speaking, however, most people are in neither of these categories. Rather, they are somewhere in the middle. With hard work, the middle group is able to learn a new language but must exert considerable effort to do so. As far as intelligence is concerned, highly intelligent people are found in all three groups.

Question 6

Why, when students finally learn English, do they rarely sound like native English speakers?

Answer

It seems that once the native language is learned, it tends to embed itself within the person. It is as if there is some kind of mechanism within the human being which works to repel the entry of a new language. Although this resistance can be overcome for the most part, battle scars tend to remain in the form of an accent. If very young children are exposed to more than a single language by native speakers of the languages, they can ultimately be expected to speak these languages as a native speaker would. Such people are referred to as "truly bilingual" or "simultaneous bilingual," as opposed to what has become known as "sequential bilingual." The term *bilingual* by itself in the minds of most denotes individuals who are conversant in more than a single language. This definition, however, does not take into account that more often than not, one of the languages used by sequential bilingual individuals is stronger than the other. As a result, the stronger or dominant language is preferred in choice situations, such as in which language to watch a movie or take a course in. More significant is the fact that the person thinks in the dominant language. On the other hand, neither language is generally dominant in a simultaneous bilingual person, who can function equally well in both languages and also think as well in one as in the other. Truly bilingual people are, of course, rarer than those who know two languages but in which one is dominant.

BIBLIOGRAPHY

Aitchison, J. (2000). *The seeds of speech: Language origin and evolution* (p.5), Cambridge, England: Cambridge University Press.

Allen, H. B. (1958). *Readings in applied English linguistics.* Appleton-Century-Crofts, Inc.

Baugh, A. & Coble, T. (2002). *A history of the English language*: NJ, Prentice Hall Inc.

Chomsky, N. (1959). Review of Verbal Behavior by B. F. Skinner, *Language, 35*, 26-58.

Corballis, M. (2008) Not the last word [Review of the book *The first word: The search for the origins of language*, by C. Kenneally]. *American Scientist, 96*(1), 68.

Culi, Y. (1988). *The Torah analogy Genesis 1*, Moznaim, New York, Jerusalem.

Finocchiaro, M. (1974). *English as a second language: From theory to practice.* New York: Regents Publishing Company.

Finocchiaro, M. & Bonomo, M. *The foreign language learner: A guide for teachers.* (1973). New York: Regents Publishing Company.

Fisher, S. R. (1999). *A history of language.* Reaktion Books, Ltd.

Fries, C. (1948). *Teaching and learning English as a foreign language.* Ann Arbor, Michigan: University of Michigan Press.

Fries, C. (1952). *The structure of English.* New York: Harcourt Brace Jovanovich.

Gelderen, E. V. (2006). *A history of the English language*. Amsterdam/Philadelphia: John

Ginsburgh, Y. (1990). *The Hebrew letters: Channels of creative consciousness*, Gal Einai, Jerusalem. Benjamins Publishing Company.

Hertz, J. H. (1990) *The Pentateuch and Haftorahs*. Second Edition. London: Soncino Press

Hirsch, S. R. Rabbi, (1990) *The Pentateuch Trumath Tzvi*. New York: Judaica Press. Hogg, Richard and Denison, David. (2006). *A history of the English language*, Cambridge Univ. Press.

Killoran, Nial. (n.d.). Old English, Anglo-Saxon (Englisc). *Omniglot, the Online Encyclopedia of Writing Systems and Language*. Retrieved from www.omniglot.com/writing/oldenglish.htm

Lado, Robert. (1957). Language across cultures. Ann Arbor, Michigan : University of Michigan Press.

Lado, Robert. (1970). *Lado English series*. NYC: Regents Publishing Company.

Lado, Robert. (1964). *Language testing*. New York: McGraw Hill.

Linguistic Society of Paris—Origin of language. Retrieved from Wikipedia.

Liberman, A. (2009). *Word origins and how we know them*. New York: Oxford Univ. Press, "Old English, Beowolf" 8.1 *Wikipedia*.

Mora, J. K. (2010). Second language teaching methods: Principles and procedures. Retrieved from http://www.moramodules.com/ALMMethods.htm

Mozeson, I. (2001). *The word: The dictionary that reveals the Hebrew source of English*. Sure Sellers Inc.

Mugglestone, L. (Ed.). (2006). *The Oxford history of English*. Oxford: Oxford University Press.

Nilsen, D. L. F. and Nilsen, A. P. (1971). *Pronunciation contrasts in English*. New York: Simon and Schuster.

Nilsen, D. (1971). The use of case grammar in teaching English as a second language. *TESOL Quarterly, 5*, 293-301.

Olender, M. (December 1977). From the language of Adam to the pluralism of Babel. *Mediterranean Historical Review,* 12 (2), 51-59.

Rivers, W. M. (1964). *The psychologist and the foreign language teacher.* TX: University of Chicago Press.

Robinett, B. W. (1978). *Teaching English to speakers of other languages.* Minneapolis: University of Minnesota Press and New York: McGraw-Hill International Book Company.

Rohde, D.L., Olson, S. & Chang J.T (2004). Modeling the recent common ancestry of all living humans. *Nature Journal, 431,* 562-566.

Ross, P.E. (1991). Hard words. *Scientific American Magazine, 264* (4), 138-147.

Skinner, B. F. (1957). *Verbal Behavior.* Acton, MA: Copley Publishing Group.

Stoynoff, S. & Chapelle, C. (2005). *ESL Tests and Testing.* Alexandria, Virginia: TESOL Pub.

Vajda, E. (2010). Linguistics 201, *The origin of language.* Also see: A replicated typo. Retrieved from http://www.replicatedtypo.com/tag/royal-linguistic-society

Viney, B. (2004) *The history of the English language.* USA: Oxford University Press.

Watts, M. H. (1998). *The Lord gave the word: A study in the history of the biblical text.* London, England: Trinitarian Bible Society.

Zintz, M. V. (1963). *Education Across Cultures.* Dubuque, Iowa: William C. Brown Book Company.

CPSIA information can be obtained at www.ICGtesting.com
Printed in the USA
LVOW06s2049211215

467401LV00018B/1338/P